Seven
Messages
to
The Mother
Church

Seven Messages to The Mother Church

MARY BAKER EDDY

*Discoverer and Founder of Christian Science
and Author of Science and Health with Key to the Scriptures*

Marcas Registradas

®

Published by

THE FIRST CHURCH OF CHRIST, SCIENTIST
in Boston, Massachusetts, U.S.A.

The facsimile of the signature of
Mary Baker Eddy and the design of
the Cross and Crown seal are trademarks
of The Christian Science Board of Directors,
registered in the United States
and other countries.

Contents

Page numbers given here refer to numbers at the bottom of the text pages. Those at the top of text pages are the original numbers, and will be useful when using a Concordance with this edition.

Foreword

In the early years of the Christian Science movement and during the unfoldment of church organization and government under the guiding hand of Mary Baker Eddy, her messages to The Mother Church were like beacons lighting the way to the establishment of the Church of Christ, Scientist. They contributed also to the evolution of its government, which is now set forth in the inspired Manual of The Mother Church.

These Messages from the Leader of the Christian Science movement to The Mother Church are as pertinent to the solution of problems today, whether they are problems of the individual or of churches, as when they were written. For this reason this compilation of seven Messages is made available in convenient form. It is hoped that from the loving counsel herein contained, all who are engaged in the activities of the Church may draw new inspiration and guidance, and so add to their spiritual equipment to carry on in all parts of the world the work of the Church of Christ, Scientist.

For those students who may wish to use a Concordance with this compilation, the original page numbers and runningheads have been retained at the top of the pages. Consecutive page numbers for this edition appear at the bottom of each page.

THE CHRISTIAN SCIENCE BOARD OF DIRECTORS

Message
to
The Mother
Church
January 2, 1898

Communion
January 2, 1898

MY BELOVED BRETHREN: — I have suggested a change in the time for holding our semi-annual church meetings, in order to separate these sessions from the excitement and commotion of the season's holidays.

In metaphysics we learn that the strength of peace and of suffering is sublime, a true, tried mental conviction that is neither tremulous nor relapsing. This strength is like the ocean, able to carry navies, yet yielding to the touch of a finger. This peace is spiritual; never selfish, stony, nor stormy, but generous, reliable, helpful, and always at hand.

Peace, like plain dealing, is somewhat out of fashion. Yet peace is desirable, and plain dealing is a jewel as beautiful as the gems that adorn the Christmas ring presented to me by my students in 1897. Few blemishes can be found in a true character, for it is always a diamond of the first water; but external gentility and good humor may be used to disguise internal vulgarity and villainy. No deformity exists in honesty, and no vulgarity in kindness. Christian Science, however, adds to these graces, and reflects the divine likeness.

Self-denial is practical, and is not only polite to all but is pleasant to those who practise it. If one would

1 follow the advice that one gratuitously bestows on
others, this would create for one's self and for the world
3 a destiny more grand than can issue from the brain of
a dreamer.

That glory only is imperishable which is fixed in one's
6 own moral make-up.

Sin is like a dock root. To cut off the top of a plant
does no good; the roots must be eradicated or the plant
9 will continue to grow. Now I am done with homilies
and, you may add, with tedious prosaics.

On the fifth of July last, my church tempted me ten-
12 derly to be proud! The deportment of its dear members
was such as to command respect everywhere. It called
forth flattering comment and created surprise in our good
15 city of Concord.

Beloved brethren, another Christmas has come and gone.
Has it enabled us to know more of the healing Christ that
18 saves from sickness and sin? Are we still searching dili-
gently to find where the young child lies, and are we satisfied to know that our sense of Truth is not demoralized,
21 finitized, cribbed, or cradled, but has risen to grasp the
spiritual idea unenvironed by materiality? Can we say
with the angels to-day: "He is risen; he is not here:
24 behold the place where they laid him"? Yes, the real
Christian Scientist can say his Christ is risen and is not
the material Christ of creeds, but is Truth, even as Jesus
27 declared; and the sense of Truth of the real Christian
Scientist is spiritualized to behold this Christ, Truth,
again healing the sick and saving sinners. The mission
30 of our Master was to all mankind, and included the very
hearts that rejected it — that refused to see the power
of Truth in healing.

Our unity and progress are proverbial, and this church's 1
gifts to me are beyond comparison — they have become
a wonder! To me, however, love is the greater marvel, 3
so I must continue to prize love even more than the gifts
which would express it. The great guerdon of divine
Love, which moves the hearts of men to goodness and 6
greatness, will reward these givers, and this encourages
me to continue to urge the perfect model for your acceptance as the ultimate of Christian Science. 9

To-day in Concord, N. H., we have a modest hall in one
of the finest localities in the city, — a reading-room and
nine other rooms in the same building. "Tell it not in 12
Gath"! I had the property bought by the courtesy of
another person to be rid of the care and responsibility of
purchasing it, and furnished him the money to pay for it. 15
The original cost of the estate was fourteen thousand
dollars. With the repairs and other necessary expenses
the amount is now about twenty thousand dollars. Ere 18
long I will see you in this hall, *Deo volente;* but my out-
door accommodations at Pleasant View are bigger than
the indoor. My little hall, which holds a trifle over two 21
hundred people, is less sufficient to receive a church of ten
thousand members than were the "five loaves and two
fishes" to feed the multitude; but the true Christian 24
Scientist is not frightened at miracles, and ofttimes small
beginnings have large endings.

Seeing that we have to attain to the ministry of right- 27
eousness in all things, we must not overlook small things
in goodness or in badness, for "trifles make perfection,"
and "the little foxes . . . spoil the vines." 30

As a peculiar people whose God is All-in-all, let us say
with St. Paul: "We faint not; but have renounced the

1 hidden things of dishonesty, not walking in craftiness, nor handling the word of God deceitfully; but by mani-
3 festation of the truth commending ourselves to every man's conscience."

(The First Church of Christ, Scientist, and Miscellany, pages 121–124)

Message
to
The Mother
Church
June, 1898

Christian Science
versus Pantheism

Christian Science
versus Pantheism

Pastor's Message to The Mother   1
Church, on the Occasion of the
June Communion, 1898   3

SUBJECT: *Not Pantheism, but Christian Science*

BELOVED brethren, since last you gathered at the
feast of our Passover, the winter winds have come   6
and gone; the rushing winds of March have shrieked and
hummed their hymns; the frown and smile of April, the
laugh of May, have fled; and the roseate blush of joyous   9
June is here and ours.

  In unctuous unison with nature, mortals are hoping and
working, putting off outgrown, wornout, or soiled gar-   12
ments — the pleasures and pains of sensation and the
sackcloth of waiting — for the springtide of Soul. For
what a man seeth he hopeth not for, but hopeth for what   15
he hath not seen, and waiteth patiently the appearing
thereof. The night is far spent, and day is not distant in
the horizon of Truth — even the day when all people   18
shall know and acknowledge one God and one Christianity.

9

1   CHRISTIAN SCIENCE NOT PANTHEISM

At this period of enlightenment, a declaration from the
3 pulpit that Christian Science is pantheism is anomalous to
those who know whereof they speak — who know that
Christian Science *is* Science, and therefore is neither
6 hypothetical nor dogmatical, but demonstrable, and
looms above the mists of pantheism higher than Mt.
Ararat above the deluge.

9   ANALYSIS OF "PANTHEISM"

According to Webster the word "pantheism" is derived from two Greek words meaning "all" and "god."
12 Webster's *derivation* of the English word "pantheism" is
most suggestive. His uncapitalized word "god" gives
the meaning of pantheism as a human opinion of "gods
15 many," or mind in matter. "The doctrine that the universe, conceived of as a whole, is God; that there is no
God but the combined forces and laws which are mani-
18 fested in the existing universe."

The Standard Dictionary has it that pantheism is the
doctrine of the deification of natural causes, conceived as
21 one personified nature, to which the religious sentiment is
directed.

Pan is a Greek prefix, but it might stand, in the term
24 pantheism, for the mythological deity of that name; and
theism for a belief concerning Deity in theology. However, Pan in imagery is preferable to pantheism in theology.

10

3   Christian Science versus Pantheism

The mythical deity may please the fancy, while pantheism   1
suits not at all the Christian sense of religion. Pan, as a
deity, is supposed to preside over sylvan solitude, and is a   3
horned and hoofed animal, half goat and half man, that
poorly presents the poetical phase of the genii of forests.[1]

My sense of nature's rich glooms is, that loneness lacks   6
but one charm to make it half divine — a friend, with
whom to whisper, "Solitude is sweet." Certain moods
of mind find an indefinable pleasure in stillness, soft,   9
silent as the storm's sudden hush; for nature's stillness
is voiced with a hum of harmony, the gentle murmur of
early morn, the evening's closing vespers, and lyre of bird   12
and brooklet.

> "O sacred solitude! divine retreat!
> Choice of the prudent! envy of the great!   15
> By thy pure stream, or in thy evening shade,
> We court fair wisdom, that celestial maid."

Theism is the belief in the personality and infinite mind   18
of one supreme, holy, self-existent God, who reveals Himself supernaturally to His creation, and whose laws are
not reckoned as science. In religion, it is a belief in one   21
God, or in many gods. It is opposed to atheism and

[1] In Roman mythology (one of my girlhood studies), Pan stood
for "universal nature proceeding from the divine Mind and provi-   24
dence, of which heaven, earth, sea, the eternal fire, are so many members." Pan was the god of shepherds and hunters, leader of the
nymphs, president of the mountains, patron of country life, and guar-   27
dian of flocks and herds. His pipe of seven reeds denotes the celestial
harmony of the seven planets; his shepherd's crook, that care and
providence by which he governs the universe; his spotted skin, the   30
stars; his goat's feet, the solidity of the earth; his man-face, the
celestial world.

11

1 monotheism, but agrees with certain forms of pantheism
and polytheism. It is the doctrine that the universe owes
3 its origin and continuity to the reason, intellect, and will of
a self-existent divine Being, who possesses all wisdom,
goodness, and power, and is the creator and preserver of
6 man.

A theistic theological belief may agree with physics and
anatomy that reason and will are properly classified as
9 mind, located in the brain; also, that the functions of
these faculties depend on conditions of matter, or brain,
for their proper exercise. But reason and will are human;
12 God is divine. In academics and in religion it is patent
that will is capable of use and of abuse, of right and wrong
action, while God is incapable of evil; that brain is matter,
15 and that there are many so-called minds; that He is the
creator of man, but that man also is a creator, making
two creators; but God is Mind and one.

18 GOD — NOT HUMAN DEVICES — THE PRESERVER
OF MAN

God, Spirit, is indeed the preserver of man. Then, in
21 the words of the Hebrew singer, "Why art thou cast down,
O my soul? and why art thou disquieted within me? hope
thou in God: for I shall yet praise Him, who is the health
24 of my countenance, and my God. . . . Who forgiveth
all thine iniquities; who healeth all thy diseases." This
being the case, what need have we of drugs, hygiene, and
27 medical therapeutics, if these are not man's preservers?
By admitting self-evident affirmations and then contra-

dicting them, monotheism is lost and pantheism is found   1
in scholastic theology. Can a single quality of God,
Spirit, be discovered in matter? The Scriptures plainly   3
declare, "The Word was God;" and "all things were
made by Him," — the Word. What, then, can matter
create, or how can it exist?   6

JESUS' DEFINITION OF EVIL

Did God create evil? or is evil self-existent, and so
possessed of the nature of God, good? Since evil is not   9
self-made, who or what hath made evil? Our Master
gave the proper answer for all time to this hoary query.
He said of evil: "Ye are of your father, the devil, and the 12
lusts of your father ye will do. He was a murderer from
the beginning, and abode not in the truth [God], because
there is no truth [reality] in him [evil]. When he speaketh 15
a lie, he speaketh of his own: for he is a liar, and the father
of it [a lie]."

Jesus' definition of devil (evil) explains evil. It shows 18
that evil is both liar and lie, a delusion and illusion. Therefore we should neither believe the lie, nor believe that it
hath embodiment or power; in other words, we should   21
not believe that a lie, nothing, can be something, but deny
it and prove its falsity. After this manner our Master cast
out evil, healed the sick, and saved sinners. Knowing   24
that evil is a lie, and, as the Scripture declares, brought
sin, sickness, and death into the world, Jesus treated the
lie summarily. He denied it, cast it out of mortal mind,   27
and thus healed sickness and sin. His treatment of evil

13

1 and disease, Science will restore and establish, — first,
because it was more effectual than all other means; and,
3 second, because evil and disease will never disappear in
any other way.

Finally, brethren, let us continue to denounce evil as the
6 illusive claim that God is not supreme, and continue to
fight it until it disappears, — but not as one that beateth
the mist, but lifteth his head above it and putteth his foot
9 upon a lie.

EVIL, AS PERSONIFIED BY THE SERPENT

Mosaic theism introduces evil, first, in the form of a
12 talking serpent, contradicting the word of God and thereby
obtaining social prestige, a large following, and changing
the order and harmony of God's creation. But the higher
15 criticism is not satisfied with this theism, and asks, If God
is *infinite* good, what and where is evil? And if Spirit
made all that was made, how can matter be an intelligent
18 creator or coworker with God? Again: Did one Mind,
or two minds, enter into the Scriptural allegory, in the
colloquy between good and evil, God and a serpent? — and
21 if two minds, what becomes of theism in Christianity? For
if God, good, is Mind, and evil also is mind, the Christian
religion has at least two Gods. If Spirit is sovereign, how
24 can matter be force or law; and if God, good, is omnipotent, what power hath evil?

It is plain that elevating evil to the altitude of mind gives
27 it power, and that the belief in more than one spirit, if

14

Spirit, God, is infinite, breaketh the First Commandment 1
in the Decalogue.

Science shows that a plurality of minds, or intelligent 3
matter, signifies more than one God, and thus prevents the
demonstration that the healing Christ, Truth, gave and
gives in proof of the omnipotence of one divine, infinite 6
Principle.

Does not the theism or belief, that after God, Spirit, had
created all things spiritually, a material creation took 9
place, and God, the preserver of man, declared that man
should die, lose the character and sovereignty of Jehovah,
and hint the gods of paganism? 12

THEISTIC RELIGIONS

We know of but three theistic religions, the Mosaic, the
Christian, and the Mohammedan. Does not each of these 15
religions mystify the absolute oneness and infinity of God,
Spirit?

A close study of the Old and New Testaments in con- 18
nection with the original text indicates, in the third chapter of Genesis, a lapse in the Mosaic religion, wherein
theism seems meaningless, or a vague apology for con- 21
tradictions. It certainly gives to matter and evil reality
and power, intelligence and law, which implies Mind,
Spirit, God; and the logical sequence of this error is idol- 24
atry — other gods.

Again: The hypothesis of mind in matter, or more than
one Mind, lapses into evil dominating good, matter govern- 27
ing Mind, and makes sin, disease, and death inevitable,

1 despite of Mind, or by the consent of Mind! Next, it
follows that the disarrangement of matter causes a man to
3 be mentally deranged; and the Babylonian sun god, moon
god, and sin god find expression in sun worship, lunacy,
sin, and mortality.

6   Does not the belief that Jesus, the man of Galilee, is
God, imply two Gods, one the divine, infinite Person, the
other a human finite personality? Does not the belief
9 that Mary was the mother of God deny the self-existence
of God? And does not the doctrine that Mohammed is
the only prophet of God infringe the sacredness of one
12 Christ Jesus?

SCIENTIFIC CHRISTIANITY MEANS ONE GOD

    Christianity, as taught and demonstrated in the first
15 century by our great Master, virtually annulled the so-
called laws of matter, idolatry, pantheism, and polytheism.
Christianity then had one God and one law, namely,
18 divine Science. It said, "Call no man your father upon
the earth, for one is your Father, which is in heaven."
Speaking of himself, Jesus said, "My Father is greater
21 than I." Christianity, as he taught and demonstrated it,
must ever rest on the basis of the First Commandment and
love for man.

24   The doctrines that embrace pantheism, polytheism, and
paganism are admixtures of matter and Spirit, truth and
error, sickness and sin, life and death. They make man
27 the servant of matter, living by reason of it, suffering because of it, and dying in consequence of it. They con-

16

stantly reiterate the belief of pantheism, that mind "sleeps   1
in the mineral, dreams in the animal, and wakes in man."

"Infinite Spirit" means one God and His creation, and   3
no reality in aught else. The term "spirits" means more
than one Spirit;—in paganism they stand for gods; in
spiritualism they imply men and women; and in Christian-   6
ity they signify a good Spirit and an evil spirit.

Is there a religion under the sun that hath demonstrated
one God and the four first rules pertaining thereto, namely,   9
"Thou shalt have no other gods before me;" "Love thy
neighbor as thyself;" "Be ye therefore perfect, even as
your Father which is in heaven is perfect;" "Whosoever   12
liveth and believeth in me shall never die." (John xi. 26.)

What mortal to-day is wise enough to do himself no
harm, to hinder not the attainment of scientific Chris-   15
tianity? Whoever demonstrates the highest humanity,—
long-suffering, self-surrender, and spiritual endeavor to
bless others,—ought to be aided, not hindered, in his   18
holy mission. I would kiss the feet of such a messenger,
for to help such a one is to help one's self. The demonstration of Christianity blesses all mankind. It loves one's   21
neighbor as one's self; it loves its enemies—and this
love benefits its enemies (though they believe it not), and
rewards its possessor; for, "If ye love them which love you,   24
what reward have ye?"

MAN THE TRUE IMAGE OF GOD

From a material standpoint, the best of people some-   27
times object to the philosophy of Christian Science, on the

1 ground that it takes away man's personality and makes
man less than man. But what saith the apostle? — even
3 this: "If a man think himself to be something, when he is
nothing, he deceiveth himself." The great Nazarene
Prophet said, "By their fruits ye shall know them:" then,
6 if the effects of Christian Science on the lives of men
be thus judged, we are sure the honest verdict of humanity will attest its uplifting power, and prevail over the
9 opposite notion that Christian Science lessens man's individuality.

The students at the Massachusetts Metaphysical Col-
12 lege, generally, were the average man and woman. But
after graduation, the best students in the class averred
that they were stronger and better than before it. With
15 twelve lessons or less, the present and future of those students had wonderfully broadened and brightened before
them, thus proving the utility of what they had been taught.
18 Christian Scientists heal functional, organic, chronic, and
acute diseases that M.D.'s have failed to heal; and,
better still, they reform desperate cases of intemperance,
21 tobacco using, and immorality, which, we regret to say,
other religious teachers are unable to effect. All this is
accomplished by the grace of God, — the effect of God
24 *understood.* A higher manhood is manifest, and never
lost, in that individual who finds the highest joy, — therefore no pleasure in loathsome habits or in sin, and no
27 necessity for disease and death. Whatever promotes
statuesque being, health, and holiness does not degrade
man's personality. Sin, sickness, appetites, and passions,
30 constitute no part of man, but obscure man. Therefore it

required the divinity of our Master to perceive the real [1]
man, and to cast out the unreal or counterfeit. It caused
St. Paul to write, — "Lie not one to another, seeing that [3]
ye have put off the old man with his deeds; and have put
on the new man, which is renewed in knowledge after
the image of Him that created him." [6]

Was our Master mistaken in judging a cause by its
effects? Shall the opinions, systems, doctrines, and dogmas of men gauge the animus of man? or shall his stature [9]
in Christ, Truth, declare him? Governed by the divine
Principle of his being, man is perfect. When will the
schools allow mortals to turn from clay to Soul for the [12]
model? The Science of being, understood and obeyed,
will demonstrate man to be superior to the best church-
member or moralist on earth, who understands not this [15]
Science. If man is spiritually fallen, it matters not what
he believes; he is not upright, and must regain his native
spiritual stature in order to be in proper shape, as certainly [18]
as the man who falls physically needs to rise again.

Mortals, content with something less than perfection —
the original standard of man — may believe that evil de- [21]
velops good, and that whatever strips off evil's disguise belittles man's personality. But God enables us to know that
evil is not the medium of good, and that good supreme de- [24]
stroys all sense of evil, obliterates the lost image that
mortals are content to call man, and demands man's un-
fallen spiritual perfectibility. [27]

The grand realism that man is the true image of God,
not fallen or inverted, is demonstrated by Christian Science.
And because Christ's dear demand, "Be ye therefore [30]

19

1 perfect," is valid, it will be found possible to fulfil it. Then
also will it be learned that good is not educed from evil,
3 but comes from the rejection of evil and its *modus operandi.*
Our scholarly expositor of the Scriptures, Lyman Abbott,
D.D., writes, "God, Spirit, is ever in universal nature."
6 Then, we naturally ask, how can Spirit be constantly passing out of mankind by death — for the universe includes
man?

THE GRANDEUR OF CHRISTIANITY

9

This closing century, and its successors, will make strong
claims on religion, and demand that the inspired Scriptural
12 commands be fulfilled. The altitude of Christianity openeth, high above the so-called laws of matter, a door that no
man can shut; it showeth to all peoples the way of escape
15 from sin, disease, and death; it lifteth the burden of sharp
experience from off the heart of humanity, and so lighteth
the path that he who entereth it may run and not weary,
18 and walk, not wait by the roadside, — yea, pass gently on
without the alterative agonies whereby the way-seeker
gains and points the path.
21 The Science of Christianity is strictly monotheism, —
it has ONE GOD. And this divine infinite Principle,
noumenon and phenomena, is demonstrably the self-
24 existent Life, Truth, Love, substance, Spirit, Mind, which
includes all that the term implies, and is all that is real and
eternal. Christian Science is irrevocable — unpierced
27 by bold conjecture's sharp point, by bald philosophy, or
by man's inventions. It is divinely true, and every hour

in time and in eternity will witness more steadfastly to its   1
practical truth. And Science is not pantheism, but Christian Science.   3

Chief among the questions herein, and nearest my
heart, is this: When shall Christianity be demonstrated
according to Christ, in these words: "Neither shall they   6
say, Lo, here! or, lo there! for, behold, the kingdom of
God is within you"?

EXHORTATION   9

Beloved brethren, the love of our loving Lord was never
more manifest than in its stern condemnation of all error,
wherever found. I counsel thee, rebuke and exhort one   12
another. Love all Christian churches for the gospel's
sake; and be exceedingly glad that the churches are united
in purpose, if not in method, to close the war between   15
flesh and Spirit, and to fight the good fight till God's will
be witnessed and done on earth as in heaven.

Sooner or later all shall know Him, recognize the great   18
truth that Spirit is infinite, and find life in Him in whom
we do "live, and move, and have our being" — life in
Life, all in All. Then shall all nations, peoples, and   21
tongues, in the words of St. Paul, have "one God and
Father of all, who is above all, and through all, and in
you all." (Ephesians iv. 6.)   24

Have I wearied you with the mysticism of opposites?
Truly there is no rest in them, and I have only traversed
my subject that you may prove for yourselves the unsub-   27

21

1 stantial nature of whatever is unlike good, weigh a sigh, and rise into the rest of righteousness with its triumphant
3 train.

Once more I write, Set your affections on things above; love one another; commune at the table of our Lord in one
6 spirit; worship in spirit and in truth; and if daily adoring, imploring, and living the divine Life, Truth, Love, thou shalt partake of the bread that cometh down from heaven,
9 drink of the cup of salvation, and be baptized in Spirit.

PRAYER FOR COUNTRY AND CHURCH

Pray for the prosperity of our country, and for her vic-
12 tory under arms; that justice, mercy, and peace continue to characterize her government, and that they shall rule all nations. Pray that the divine presence may still guide and
15 bless our chief magistrate, those associated with his executive trust, and our national judiciary; give to our congress wisdom, and uphold our nation with the right arm of His
18 righteousness.

In your peaceful homes remember our brave soldiers, whether in camp or in battle.[1] Oh, may their love of coun-
21 try, and their faithful service thereof, be unto them life-preservers! May the divine Love succor and protect them, as at Manila, where brave men, led by the dauntless
24 Dewey, and shielded by the power that saved them, sailed victoriously through the jaws of death and blotted out the Spanish squadron.
27 Great occasion have we to rejoice that our nation, which

---

[1] This refers to the war between United States and Spain for the liberty of Cuba.

fed her starving foe, — already murdering her peaceful ₁
seamen and destroying millions of her money, — will be
as formidable in war as she has been compassionate in ₃
peace.

May our Father-Mother God, who in times past hath
spread for us a table in the wilderness and "in the midst ₆
of our enemies," establish us in the most holy faith, plant
our feet firmly on Truth, the rock of Christ, the "substance
of things hoped for" — and fill us with the life and under- ₉
standing of God, and good will towards men.

MARY BAKER EDDY

23

Message
to
The Mother
Church

June 4, 1899

Communion
June 4, 1899

My Beloved Brethren: — Looking on this annual assem- 6
blage of human consciousness, — health, harmony, growth,
grandeur, and achievement, garlanded with glad faces,
willing hands, and warm hearts, — who would say to-day, 9
"What a fond fool is hope"? The fruition of friendship,
the world's arms outstretched to us, heart meeting heart
across continents and oceans, bloodless sieges and tear- 12
less triumphs, the "well done" already yours, and the
undone waiting only your swift hands, — these are
enough to make this hour glad. What more abounds 15
and abides in the hearts of these hearers and speakers,
pen may not tell.

Nature reflects man and art pencils him, but it remains 18
for Science to reveal man to man; and between these lines
of thought is written in luminous letters, O man, what
art thou? Where art thou? Whence and whither? And 21
what shall the answer be? Expressive silence, or with
finger pointing upward, — Thither! Then produce thy
records, time-table, log, traveller's companion, *et cetera*, 24
and prove fairly the facts relating to the thitherward, —
the rate of speed, the means of travel, and the number
en route. Now what have you learned? The mystery 27
of godliness — God made "manifest in the flesh," seen
of men, and spiritually understood; and the mystery of
iniquity — how to separate the tares from the wheat, 30
that they consume in their own fires and no longer

27

1 kindle altars for human sacrifice. Have you learned to
conquer sin, false affections, motives, and aims, — to be
3 not only sayers but doers of the law?

Brethren, our annual meeting is a grave guardian. It
requires you to report progress, to refresh memory, to
6 rejuvenate the branches and to vivify the buds, to bend
upward the tendrils and to incline the vine towards the
parent trunk. You come from feeding your flocks, big
9 with promise; and you come with the sling of Israel's
chosen one to meet the Goliaths.

I have only to dip my pen in my heart to say, All honor
12 to the members of our Board of Lectureship connected
with The Mother Church. Loyal to the divine Principle
they so ably vindicate, they earn their laurels. History
15 will record their words, and their works will follow
them. When reading their lectures, I have felt the touch
of the spirit of the Mars' Hill orator, which always
18 thrills the soul.

The members of the Board of Education, under the
auspices of the Massachusetts Metaphysical College, have
21 acquitted themselves nobly. The students in my last
class in 1898 are stars in my crown of rejoicing.

We are deeply grateful that the church militant is
24 looking into the subject of Christian Science, for Zion
must put on her beautiful garments — her bridal robes.
The hour is come; the bride (Word) is adorned, and lo,
27 the bridegroom cometh! Are our lamps trimmed and
burning?

The doom of the Babylonish woman, referred to in Reve-
30 lation, is being fulfilled. This woman, "drunken with the
blood of the saints, and with the blood of the martyrs
of Jesus," "drunk with the wine of her fornication,"

would enter even the church, — the body of Christ, Truth; 1
and, retaining the heart of the harlot and the purpose
of the destroying angel, would pour wormwood into the 3
waters — the disturbed human mind — to drown the
strong swimmer struggling for the shore, — aiming for
Truth, — and if possible, to poison such as drink of the 6
living water. But the recording angel, standing with
"right foot upon the sea, and his left foot on the earth,"
has in his hand a book open (ready to be read), which un- 9
covers and kills this mystery of iniquity and interprets the
mystery of godliness, — how the first is finished and the
second is no longer a mystery or a miracle, but a marvel, 12
casting out evil and healing the sick. And a voice was
heard, saying, "Come out of her, my people" (hearken
not to her lies), "that ye receive not of her plagues. For 15
her sins have reached unto heaven, and God hath remem-
bered her iniquities . . . double unto her double according to her works: in the cup which she hath filled fill 18
to her double . . . for she saith in her heart, I . . . am
no widow, . . . Therefore shall her plagues come in one
day, death, and mourning, and famine; . . . for strong is 21
the Lord God who judgeth her." That which the Revelator saw in spiritual vision will be accomplished. The
Babylonish woman is fallen, and who should mourn 24
over the widowhood of lust, of her that "is become the
habitation of devils, and the hold of every foul spirit,
and a cage of every unclean . . . bird"? 27

One thing is eternally here; it reigns supreme to-day,
to-morrow, forever. We need it in our homes, at our fire-
sides, on our altars, for with it win we the race of the 30
centuries. We have it only as we live it. This is that
needful one thing — divine Science, whereby thought is

1 *spiritualized*, reaching outward and upward to Science in
Christianity, Science in medicine, in physics, and in
3 metaphysics.

Happy are the people whose God is All-in-all, who ask
only to be judged according to their works, who live to
6 love. We thank the Giver of all good for the marvellous
speed of the chariot-wheels of Truth and for the steadfast,
calm coherence in the ranks of Christian Science.

9 On comparison, it will be found that Christian Science
possesses more of Christ's teachings and example than
all other religions since the first century. Comparing
12 our scientific system of metaphysical therapeutics with
materia medica, we find that divine metaphysics com-
pletely overshadows and overwhelms *materia medica*, even
15 as Aaron's rod swallowed up the rods of the magicians
of Egypt. I deliberately declare that when I was in practice, out of one hundred cases I healed ninety-nine to
18 the ten of *materia medica.*

We should thank God for persecution and for prosecu-
tion, if from these ensue a purer Protestantism and mono-
21 theism for the latter days of the nineteenth century. A
siege of the combined centuries, culminating in fierce attack,
cannot demolish our strongholds. The forts of Christian
24 Science, garrisoned by God's chosen ones, can never sur-
render. Unlike Russia's armament, ours is not costly as
men count cost, but it is rich beyond price, staunch and
27 indestructible on land or sea; it is not curtailed in peace,
surrendered in conquest, nor laid down at the feet of
progress through the hands of omnipotence. And why?
30 Because it is "on earth peace, good will toward men," —
a cover and a defence adapted to all men, all nations,
all times, climes, and races. I cannot quench my

desire to say this; and words are not vain when the 1
depth of desire can find no other outlet to liberty.
"Therefore . . . let us go on unto perfection; not laying 3
again the foundation of repentance from dead works."
(Hebrews 6 : 1.)

A coroner's inquest, a board of health, or class legisla- 6
tion is less than the Constitution of the United States, and
infinitely less than God's benign government, which is
"no respecter of persons." Truth crushed to earth springs 9
spontaneously upward, and whispers to the breeze man's
inalienable birthright — *Liberty*. "Where the Spirit of
the Lord is, there is liberty." God is everywhere. No 12
crown nor sceptre nor rulers rampant can quench the vital
heritage of freedom — man's right to adopt a religion,
to employ a physician, to live or to die according to the 15
dictates of his own rational conscience and enlightened
understanding. Men cannot punish a man for suicide;
God does that. 18

Christian Scientists abide by the laws of God and the
laws of the land; and, following the command of the
Master, they go into all the world, preaching the gospel 21
and healing the sick. Therefore be wise and harmless, for
without the former the latter were impracticable. A lack
of wisdom betrays Truth into the hands of evil as effec- 24
tually as does a subtle conspirator; the motive is not as
wicked, but the result is as injurious. Return not evil for
evil, but "overcome evil with good." Then, whatever 27
the shaft aimed at you or your practice may be, it will
fall powerless, and God will reward your enemies according to their works. Watch, and pray daily that evil 30
suggestions, in whatever guise, take no root in your
thought nor bear fruit. Ofttimes examine yourselves, and

31

1 see if there be found anywhere a deterrent of Truth and
Love, and "hold fast that which is good."

3   I reluctantly foresee great danger threatening our nation,—imperialism, monopoly, and a lax system of religion. But the spirit of humanity, ethics, and Christianity
6 sown broadcast—all concomitants of Christian Science
—is taking strong hold of the public thought throughout our beloved country and in foreign lands, and is
9 tending to counteract the trend of mad ambition.

   There is no night but in God's frown; there is no day
but in His smile. The oracular skies, the verdant earth
12 —bird, brook, blossom, breeze, and balm—are richly
fraught with divine reflection. They come at Love's call.
The nod of Spirit is nature's natal.

15   And how is man, seen through the lens of Spirit,
enlarged, and how counterpoised his origin from dust,
and how he presses to his original, never severed
18 from Spirit! O ye who leap disdainfully from this rock
of ages, return and plant thy steps in Christ, Truth,
"the stone which the builders rejected"! Then will
21 angels administer grace, do thy errands, and be thy
dearest allies. The divine law gives to man health
and life everlasting—gives a soul to Soul, a present
24 harmony wherein the good man's heart takes hold on
heaven, and whose feet can never be moved. These
are His green pastures beside still waters, where faith
27 mounts upward, expatiates, strengthens, and exults.

   Lean not too much on your Leader. Trust God to
direct your steps. Accept my counsel and teachings only
30 as they include the spirit and the letter of the Ten Commandments, the Beatitudes, and the teachings and
example of Christ Jesus. Refrain from public contro-

versy; correct the false with the true — then leave the 1
latter to propagate. Watch and guard your own thoughts
against evil suggestions and against malicious mental 3
malpractice, wholly disloyal to the teachings of Christian
Science. This hidden method of committing crime —
socially, physically, and morally — will ere long be un- 6
earthed and punished as it deserves. The effort of
disloyal students to blacken me and to keep my works
from public recognition — students seeking only public 9
notoriety, whom I have assisted pecuniarily and striven to
uplift morally — has been made too many times and has
failed too often for me to fear it. The spirit of Truth is 12
the lever which elevates mankind. I have neither the
time nor the inclination to be continually pursuing a lie
— the one evil or the evil one. Therefore I ask the help 15
of others in this matter, and I ask that according to
the Scriptures my students reprove, rebuke, and exhort.
A lie left to itself is not so soon destroyed as it is with 18
the help of truth-telling. Truth never falters nor fails;
it is our faith that fails.

All published quotations from my works must have 21
the author's name added to them. Quotation-marks are
not sufficient. Borrowing from my copyrighted works,
without credit, is inadmissible. But I need not say this 24
to the loyal Christian Scientist — to him who keeps
the commandments. "Science and Health with Key to
the Scriptures" has an enormous strain put upon it, 27
being used as a companion to the Bible in all your
public ministrations, as teacher and as the embodiment
and substance of the truth that is taught; hence 30
my request, that you borrow little else from it, should
seem reasonable.

1   Beloved, that which purifies the affections also strengthens them, removes fear, subdues sin, and endues with
3 divine power; that which refines character at the same
time humbles, exalts, and commands a man, and obedience
gives him courage, devotion, and attainment. For this
6 hour, for this period, for spiritual sacrament, sacrifice,
and ascension, we unite in giving thanks. For the body
of Christ, for the life that we commemorate and would
9 emulate, for the bread of heaven whereof if a man eat
"he shall live forever," for the cup red with loving resti-
tution, redemption, and inspiration, we give thanks. The
12 signet of the great heart, given to me in a little symbol,
seals the covenant of everlasting love. May apostate
praise return to its first love, above the symbol seize the
15 spirit, speak the "new tongue" — and may thought soar
and Soul be.

*(The First Church of Christ, Scientist, and Miscellany,
pages 124–131)*

34

Message
to
The Mother Church

June, 1900

Message for 1900

MY beloved brethren, methinks even I am touched 1
with the tone of your happy hearts, and can see
your glad faces, aglow with gratitude, chinked within the 3
storied walls of The Mother Church. If, indeed, we may
be absent from the body and present with the ever-present
Love filling all space, time, and immortality — then I am 6
with thee, heart answering to heart, and mine to thine in
the glow of divine reflection.

I am grateful to say that in the last year of the nine- 9
teenth century this first church of our denomination,
chartered in 1879, is found crowned with unprecedented
prosperity; a membership of over sixteen thousand com- 12
municants in unity, with rapidly increasing numbers, rich
spiritual attainments, and right convictions fast forming
themselves into conduct. 15

Christian Science already has a hearing and following
in the five grand divisions of the globe; in Australia, the
Philippine Islands, Hawaiian Islands; and in most of the 18
principal cities, such as Boston, New York, Philadelphia,
Washington, Baltimore, Charleston, S. C., Atlanta, New
Orleans, Chicago, St. Louis, Denver, Salt Lake City, San 21
Francisco, Montreal, London, Edinburgh, Dublin, Paris,
Berlin, Rome, Pekin. Judging from the number of the
readers of my books and those interested in them, over a 24

1 million of people are already interested in Christian
Science; and this interest increases. Churches of this
3 denomination are springing up in the above-named cities,
and, thanks to God, the people most interested in this
old-new theme of redeeming Love are among the best people
6 on earth and in heaven.

The song of Christian Science is, "Work — work —
work — watch and pray." The close observer reports
9 three types of human nature — the right thinker and
worker, the idler, and the intermediate.

The right thinker works; he gives little time to society
12 manners or matters, and benefits society by his example
and usefulness. He takes no time for amusement, ease,
frivolity; he earns his money and gives it wisely to the
15 world.

The wicked idler earns little and is stingy; he has
plenty of means, but he uses them evilly. Ask how he
18 gets his money, and his satanic majesty is supposed to
answer smilingly: "By cheating, lying, and crime; his
dupes are his capital; his stock in trade, the wages of sin;
21 your idlers are my busiest workers; they will leave a
lucrative business to work for me." Here we add: The
doom of such workers will come, and it will be more sudden,
24 severe, and lasting than the adversary can hope.

The intermediate worker works at times. He says:
"It is my duty to take some time for myself; however, I
27 believe in working when it is convenient." Well, all that
is good. But what of the fruits of your labors? And he
answers: "I am not so successful as I could wish, but I
30 work hard enough to be so."

Now, what saith Christian Science? "When a man is 1
right, his thoughts are right, active, and they are fruitful;
he loses self in love, and cannot hear himself, unless he 3
loses the chord. The right thinker and worker does his
best, and does the thinking for the ages. No hand that
feels not his help, no heart his comfort. He improves 6
moments; to him time is money, and he hoards this capital
to distribute gain."

If the right thinker and worker's servitude is duly valued, 9
he is not thereby worshipped. One's idol is by no means
his servant, but his master. And they who love a good
work or good workers are themselves workers who appre- 12
ciate a life, and labor to awake the slumbering capability
of man. And what the best thinker and worker has said
and done, they are not far from saying and doing. As a 15
rule the Adam-race are not apt to worship the pioneer
of spiritual ideas, — but ofttimes to shun him as their
tormentor. Only the good man loves the right thinker 18
and worker, and cannot worship him, for that would destroy this man's goodness.

To-day it surprises us that during the period of captivity 21
the Israelites in Babylon hesitated not to call the divine
name Yahwah, afterwards transcribed Jehovah; also
that women's names contained this divine appellative and 24
so sanctioned idolatry, — other gods. In the heathen
conception Yahwah, misnamed Jehovah, was a god of
hate and of love, who repented himself, improved on his 27
work of creation, and revenged himself upon his enemies.
However, the animus of heathen religion was not the in-
centive of the devout Jew — but has it not tainted the reli- 30

1 gious sects? This seedling misnomer couples love and
hate, good and evil, health and sickness, life and death,
3 with man — makes His opposites as real and normal as
the one God, and so unwittingly consents to many minds
and many gods. This precedent that would commingle
6 Christianity, the gospel of the New Testament and the
teaching of the righteous Galilean, Christ Jesus, with the
Babylonian and Neoplatonic religion, is being purged by
9 a purer Judaism and nearer approach to monotheism and
the perfect worship of one God.

To-day people are surprised at the new and forward
12 steps in religion, which indicate a renaissance greater than
in the mediæval period; but ought not this to be an agree-
able surprise, inasmuch as these are progressive signs of
15 thè times?

It should seem rational that the only perfect religion is
divine Science, Christianity as taught by our great Master;
18 that which leaves the beaten path of human doctrines and
is the truth of God, and of man and the universe. The
divine Principle and rules of this Christianity being de-
21 monstrable, they are undeniable; and they must be found
final, absolute, and eternal. The question as to religion
is: Does it demonstrate its doctrines? Do religionists
24 believe that God is *One* and *All?* Then whatever is real
must proceed from God, from Mind, and is His reflection
and Science. Man and the universe coexist with God in
27 Science, and they reflect God and nothing else. In divine
Science, divine Love includes and reflects all that really
is, all personality and individuality. St. Paul beautifully
30 enunciates this fundamental fact of Deity as the "Father

of all, who is above all, and through all, and in you all." 1
This scientific statement of the origin, nature, and government of all things coincides with the First Commandment 3
of the Decalogue, and leaves no opportunity for idolatry
or aught besides God, good. It gives evil no origin, no
reality. Here note the words of our Master corroborating 6
this as self-evident. Jesus said the opposite of God —
good — named devil — evil — "is a liar, and the father
of it" — that is, its origin is a myth, a lie. 9

Applied to Deity, Father and Mother are synonymous
terms; they signify one God. Father, Son, and Holy
Ghost mean God, man, and divine Science. God is self- 12
existent, the essence and source of the two latter, and their
office is that of eternal, infinite individuality. I see no
other way under heaven and among men whereby to have 15
one God, and man in His image and likeness, loving another as himself. This being the divine Science of divine
Love, it would enable man to escape from idolatry of 18
every kind, to obey the First Commandment of the Decalogue: "Thou shalt have no other gods before me;"
and the command of Christ: "Love thy neighbor as thy- 21
self." On this rock Christian Science is built. It may
be the rock which the builders reject for a season; but
it is the Science of God and His universe, and it will be- 24
come the head of the corner, the foundation of all systems
of religion.

The spiritual sense of the Scriptures understood enables 27
one to utilize the power of divine Love in casting out God's
opposites, called evils, and in healing the sick. Not mad-
ness, but might and majesty attend every footstep of 30

41

1 Christian Science. There is no imperfection, no lack in
the Principle and rules which demonstrate it. Only the
3 demonstrator can mistake or fail in proving its power and
divinity. In the words of St. Paul: "I count not myself
to have apprehended: but this one thing I do, forgetting
6 those things which are behind, and reaching forth to those
things which are before, I press toward the mark for the
prize of the high calling of God in Christ Jesus" — in the
9 true idea of God. Any mystery in Christian Science de-
parts when dawns the spiritual meaning thereof; and the
spiritual sense of the Scriptures is the scientific sense which
12 interprets the healing Christ. A child can measurably
understand Christian Science, for, through his simple faith
and purity, he takes in its spiritual sense that puzzles the
15 man. The child not only accepts Christian Science more
readily than the adult, but he practises it. This notable
fact proves that the so-called fog of this Science obtains
18 not in the Science, but in the material sense which the
adult entertains of it. However, to a man who uses tobacco, is profane, licentious, and breaks God's com-
21 mandments, that which destroys his false appetites and
lifts him from the stubborn thrall of sin to a meek and
loving disciple of Christ, clothed and in his right mind, is
24 not darkness but light.

Again, that Christian Science is the Science of God is
proven when, in the degree that you accept it, understand
27 and practise it, you are made better physically, morally,
and spiritually. Some modern exegesis on the prophetic
Scriptures cites 1875 as the year of the second coming of
30 Christ. In that year the Christian Science textbook,

42

"Science and Health with Key to the Scriptures," was 1
first published. From that year the United States official
statistics show the annual death-rate to have gradually 3
diminished. Likewise the religious sentiment has in-
creased; creeds and dogmas have been sifted, and a
greater love of the Scriptures manifested. In 1895 it was 6
estimated that during the past three years there had been
more Bibles sold than in all the other 1893 years. Many
of our best and most scholarly men and women, distin- 9
guished members of the bar and bench, press and pulpit,
and those in all the walks of life, will tell you they never
loved the Bible and appreciated its worth as they did after 12
reading "Science and Health with Key to the Scriptures."
This is my great reward for having suffered, lived, and
learned, in a small degree, the Science of perfectibility 15
through Christ, the Way, the Truth, and the Life.

Is there more than one Christ, and hath Christ a second
appearing? There is but one Christ. And from ever- 18
lasting to everlasting this Christ is never absent. In doubt
and darkness we say as did Mary of old: "I know not
where they have laid him." But when we behold the 21
Christ walking the wave of earth's troubled sea, like Peter
we believe in the second coming, and would walk more
closely with Christ; but find ourselves so far from the em- 24
bodiment of Truth that ofttimes this attempt measurably
fails, and we cry, "Save, or I perish!" Then the tender,
loving Christ is found near, affords help, and we are saved 27
from our fears. Thus it is we walk here below, and wait
for the full appearing of Christ till the long night is past
and the morning dawns on eternal day. Then, if sin and 30

1 flesh are put off, we shall know and behold more nearly
the embodied Christ, and with saints and angels shall be
3 satisfied to go on till we awake in his likeness.

The good man imparts knowingly and unknowingly
goodness; but the evil man also exhales consciously and
6 unconsciously his evil nature — hence, be careful of your
company. As in the floral kingdom odors emit character-
istics of tree and flower, a perfume or a poison, so the hu-
9 man character comes forth a blessing or a bane upon
individuals and society. A wicked man has little real
intelligence; he may steal other people's good thoughts,
12 and wear the purloined garment as his own, till God's
discipline takes it off for his poverty to appear.

Our Master saith to his followers: "Bring forth things
15 new and old." In this struggle remember that sensitive-
ness is sometimes selfishness, and that mental idleness or
apathy is always egotism and animality. Usefulness is
18 doing rightly by yourself and others. We lose a percentage
due to our activity when doing the work that belongs to
another. When a man begins to quarrel with himself he
21 stops quarrelling with others. We must exterminate self
before we can successfully war with mankind. Then, at
last, the right will boil over the brim of life and the fire
24 that purifies sense with Soul will be extinguished. It is not
Science for the wicked to wallow or the good to weep.

Learn to obey; but learn first what obedience is.
27 When God speaks to you through one of His little ones,
and you obey the mandate but retain a desire to follow
your own inclinations, that is not obedience. I some-
30 times advise students not to do certain things which I

know it were best not to do, and they comply with my 1
counsel; but, watching them, I discern that this obedience
is contrary to their inclination. Then I sometimes with- 3
draw that advice and say: "You may do it if you desire." But I say this not because it is the best thing to
do, but because the student is not willing — therefore, 6
not ready — to obey.

The secret of Christian Science in right thinking and
acting is open to mankind, but few, comparatively, see it; 9
or, seeing it, shut their eyes and wait for a more convenient
season; or as of old cry out: "Why art thou come hither
to torment me before the time?"   12

Strong desires bias human judgment and misguide action, else they uplift them. But the reformer continues
his lightning, thunder, and sunshine till the mental at- 15
mosphere is clear. The reformer must be a hero at all
points, and he must have conquered himself before he can
conquer others. Sincerity is more successful than genius 18
or talent.

The twentieth century in the ebb and flow of thought
will challenge the thinkers, speakers, and workers to do 21
their best. Whosoever attempts to ostracize Christian
Science will signally fail; for no one can fight against God,
and win.   24

My loyal students will tell you that for many years I
have desired to step aside and to have some one take my
place as leader of this mighty movement. Also that I 27
strove earnestly to fit others for this great responsibility.
But no one else has seemed equal to "bear the burden and
heat of the day."   30

1 Success in sin is downright defeat. Hatred bites the
heel of love that is treading on its head. All that worketh
3 good is some manifestation of God asserting and developing good. Evil is illusion, that after a fight vanisheth with
the new birth of the greatest and best. Conflict and perse-
6 cution are the truest signs that can be given of the greatness
of a cause or of an individual, provided this warfare is
honest and a world-imposed struggle. Such conflict never
9 ends till unconquerable right is begun anew, and hath
gained fresh energy and final victory.

Certain elements in human nature would undermine
12 the civic, social, and religious rights and laws of nations
and peoples, striking at liberty, human rights, and self-
government — and this, too, in the name of God, justice,
15 and humanity! These elements assail even the new-old
doctrines of the prophets and of Jesus and his disciples.
History shows that error repeats itself until it is extermi-
18 nated. Surely the wisdom of our forefathers is not added
but subtracted from whatever sways the sceptre of self and
pelf over individuals, weak provinces, or peoples. Here
21 our hope anchors in God who reigns, and justice and judgment are the habitation of His throne forever.

Only last week I received a touching token of unselfed
24 manhood from a person I never saw. But since publishing
this page I have learned it was a private soldier who sent
to me, in the name of a first lieutenant of the United States
27 infantry in the Philippine Islands, ten five-dollar gold
pieces snuggled in Pears' soap. Surely it is enough for a
soldier serving his country in that torrid zone to part with
30 his soap, but to send me some of his hard-earned money

cost me a tear! Yes, and it gave me more pleasure than 1
millions of money could have given.

Beloved brethren, have no discord over music. Hold 3
in yourselves the true sense of harmony, and this sense
will harmonize, unify, and unself you. Once I was pas-
sionately fond of material music, but jarring elements 6
among musicians weaned me from this love and wedded
me to spiritual music, the music of Soul. Thus it is with
whatever turns mortals away from earth to heaven; we 9
have the promise that "all things work together for good
to them that love God," — love good. The human sigh
for peace and love is answered and compensated by divine 12
love. Music is more than sound in unison. The deaf
Beethoven besieges you with tones intricate, profound,
commanding. Mozart rests you. To me his composition 15
is the triumph of art, for he measures himself against
deeper grief. I want not only quality, quantity, and vari-
ation in tone, but the unction of Love. Music is divine. 18
Mind, not matter, makes music; and if the divine tone be
lacking, the human tone has no melody for me. Adelaide
A. Proctor breathes my thought: — 21

> It flooded the crimson twilight
>   Like the close of an angel's psalm,
> And it lay on my fevered spirit   24
>   With a touch of infinite calm.

In Revelation St. John refers to what "the Spirit saith
unto the churches." His allegories are the highest criticism 27
on all human action, type, and system. His symbolic
ethics bravely rebuke lawlessness. His types of purity

1 pierce corruption beyond the power of the pen. They are
bursting paraphrases projected from divinity upon human-
3 ity, the spiritual import whereof "holdeth the seven stars
in His right hand and walketh in the midst of the seven
golden candlesticks" — the radiance of glorified Being.

6   In Revelation, second chapter, his messages to the
churches commence with the church of Ephesus. History
records Ephesus as an illustrious city, the capital of Asia
9 Minor. It especially flourished as an emporium in the
time of the Roman Emperor Augustus. St. Paul's life
furnished items concerning this city. Corresponding to
12 its roads, its gates, whence the Ephesian elders travelled to
meet St. Paul, led northward and southward. At the head
of the harbor was the temple of Diana, the tutelary divinity
15 of Ephesus. The earlier temple was burned on the night
that Alexander the Great was born. Magical arts pre-
vailed at Ephesus; hence the Revelator's saying: "I
18 have somewhat against thee, because thou hast left thy
first love . . . and will remove thy candlestick out of his
place, except thou repent." This prophecy has been ful-
21 filled. Under the influence of St. Paul's preaching the
magical books in that city were publicly burned. It were
well if we had a St. Paul to purge our cities of charlatanism.
24 During St. Paul's stay in that city — over two years — he
labored in the synagogue, in the school of Tyrannus, and
also in private houses. The entire city is now in ruins.

27   The Revelation of St. John in the apostolic age is symbolic, rather than personal or historical. It refers to the
Hebrew Balaam as the devourer of the people. Nicolaitan
30 church presents the phase of a great controversy, ready to

destroy the unity and the purity of the church. It is said 1
"a controversy was inevitable when the Gentiles entered
the church of Christ" in that city. The Revelator com- 3
mends the church at Ephesus by saying: "Thou hatest
the deeds of the Nicolaitanes, which I also hate." It is
written of this church that their words were brave and their 6
deeds evil. The orgies of their idolatrous feasts and their
impurities were part of a system supported by their doctrine and their so-called prophetic illumination. Their 9
distinctive feature the apostle justly regards as heathen,
and so he denounces the Nicolaitan church.

Alexander the Great founded the city of Smyrna, and 12
after a series of wars it was taken and sacked. The Revelator writes of this church of Smyrna: "Be thou faithful
unto death, and I will give thee a crown of life." A glad 15
promise to such as wait and weep.

The city of Pergamos was devoted to a sensual worship.
There Æsculapius, the god of medicine, acquired fame; 18
and a serpent was the emblem of Æsculapius. Its medical
practice included charms and incantations. The Revelator refers to the church in this city as dwelling "where 21
Satan's seat is." The Pergamene church consisted of the
school of Balaam and Æsculapius, idolatry and medicine.

The principal deity in the city of Thyatira was Apollo. 24
Smith writes: "In this city the amalgamation of different
pagan religions seems not to have been wholly discoun-
tenanced by the authorities of the Judæo-Christian 27
church."

The Revelator speaks of the angel of the church in
Philadelphia as being bidden to write the approval of this 30

1 church by our Master — he saith: "Thou hast a little
strength, and hast kept my word, and hast not denied my
3 name. Behold, I will make them of the synagogue of
Satan . . . to know that I have loved thee. . . . Hold
that fast which thou hast, that no man take thy crown."
6 He goes on to portray seven churches, the full number
of days named in the creation, which signifies a complete
time or number of whatever is spoken of in the Scriptures.
9 Beloved, let him that hath an ear (that discerneth spiritually) hear what the Spirit saith unto the churches; and
seek thou the divine import of the Revelator's vision —
12 and no other. Note his inspired rebuke to all the churches
except the church in Philadelphia — the name whereof
signifies "brotherly love." I call your attention to this
15 to remind you of the joy you have had in following the
more perfect way, or Golden Rule: "As ye would that
men should do to you, do ye." Let no root of bitterness
18 spring up among you, but hold in your full hearts fervently
the charity that seeketh not only her own, but another's
good. The angel that spake unto the churches cites Jesus
21 as "he that hath the key of David; that openeth and no
man shutteth, and shutteth and no man openeth;" in
other words, he that toiled for the spiritually indispensable.
24 At all times respect the character and philanthropy of
the better class of M.D.'s — and if you are stoned from
the pulpit, say in your heart as the devout St. Stephen said:
27 "Lord, lay not this sin to their charge."

When invited to a feast you naturally ask who are to be
the guests. And being told they are distinguished indi-
30 viduals, you prepare accordingly for the festivity. Putting

aside the old garment, you purchase, at whatever price, a   1
new one that is up to date. To-day you have come to a
sumptuous feast, to one that for many years has been await-   3
ing you. The guests are distinguished above human title
and this feast is a Passover. To sit at this table of their
Lord and partake of what divine Love hath prepared for   6
them, Christian Scientists start forward with true ambition. The Passover, spiritually discerned, is a wonderful
passage over a tear-filled sea of repentance — which of   9
all human experience is the most divine; and after this
Passover cometh victory, faith, and good works.

When a supercilious consciousness that saith "there is 12
no sin," has awakened to see through sin's disguise the
claim of sin, and thence to see that sin has no claim, it
yields to sharp conviction — it sits in sackcloth — it waits 15
in the desert — and fasts in the wilderness. But all this
time divine Love has been preparing a feast for this
awakened consciousness. To-day you have come to Love's 18
feast, and you kneel at its altar. May you have on a wed-
ding garment new and old, and the touch of the hem of
this garment heal the sick and the sinner!   21

In the words of St. John, may the angel of The Mother
Church write of this church: "Thou hast not left thy first
love, I know thy works, and charity, and service, and faith, 24
and thy patience, and thy works; and the last to be more
than the first."

Watch! till the storms are o'er —   27
  The cold blasts done,
The reign of heaven begun,
  And love, the evermore.   30

Message
to
The Mother Church
June, 1901

Message for 1901

Beloved brethren, to-day I extend my heart-and-hand-fellowship to the faithful, to those whose hearts have been beating through the mental avenues of mankind for God and humanity; and rest assured you can never lack God's outstretched arm so long as you are in His service. Our first communion in the new century finds Christian Science more extended, more rapidly advancing, better appreciated, than ever before, and nearer the whole world's acceptance.

To-day you meet to commemorate in unity the life of our Lord, and to rise higher and still higher in the individual consciousness most essential to your growth and usefulness; to add to your treasures of thought the great realities of being, which constitute mental and physical perfection. The baptism of the Spirit, and the refreshment and invigoration of the human in communion with the Divine, have brought you hither.

All that is true is a sort of necessity, a portion of the primal reality of things. Truth comes from a deep sincerity that must always characterize heroic hearts; it is the better side of man's nature developing itself.

As Christian Scientists you seek to define God to your own consciousness by feeling and applying the nature and practical possibilities of divine Love: to gain the absolute

55

1 and supreme certainty that Christianity is now what Christ
Jesus taught and demonstrated — health, holiness, im-
3 mortality. The highest spiritual Christianity in individual
lives is indispensable to the acquiring of greater power in
the perfected Science of healing all manner of diseases.

6 We know the healing standard of Christian Science was
and is traduced by trying to put into the *old* garment the
new-old cloth of Christian healing. To attempt to twist
9 the fatal magnetic element of human will into harmony
with divine power, or to substitute good words for good
deeds, a fair seeming for right being, may suit the weak or
12 the worldly who find the standard of Christ's healing too
high for them. Absolute certainty in the practice of divine
metaphysics constitutes its utility, since it has a divine and
15 demonstrable Principle and rule — if some fall short of
Truth, others will attain it, and these are they who will
adhere to it. The feverish pride of sects and systems is
18 the death's-head at the feast of Love, but Christianity is
ever storming sin in its citadels, blessing the poor in spirit
and keeping peace with God.

21 What Jesus' disciples of old experienced, his followers
of to-day will prove, namely, that a departure from the
direct line in Christ costs a return under difficulties; dark-
24 ness, doubt, and unrequited toil will beset all their return-
ing footsteps. Only a firm foundation in Truth can give
a fearless wing and a sure reward.

27 The history of Christian Science explains its rapid
growth. In my church of over twenty-one thousand six
hundred and thirty-one communicants (two thousand four
30 hundred and ninety-six of whom have been added since

last November) there spring spontaneously the higher hope, 1
and increasing virtue, fervor, and fidelity. The special
benediction of our Father-Mother God rests upon this 3
hour: "Blessed are ye when men shall revile you, and persecute you, and shall say all manner of evil against you
falsely, for my sake." 6

GOD IS THE INFINITE PERSON

We hear it said the Christian Scientists have no God
because their God is not a person. Let us examine this. 9
The loyal Christian Scientists absolutely adopt Webster's
definition of God, "A Supreme Being," and the Standard
dictionary's definition of God, "The one Supreme Being, 12
self-existent and eternal." Also, we accept God, emphati-
cally, in the higher definition derived from the Bible, and
this accords with the literal sense of the lexicons: "God is 15
Spirit," "God is Love." Then, to define Love in divine
Science we use this phrase for God — divine Principle.
By this we mean Mind, a permanent, fundamental, intel- 18
ligent, divine Being, called in Scripture, Spirit, Love.

It is sometimes said: "God is Love, but this is no argu-
ment that Love is God; for God is light, but light is not 21
God." The first proposition is correct, and is not lost
by the conclusion, for Love expresses the nature of God;
but the last proposition does not illustrate the first, as 24
light, being matter, loses the nature of God, Spirit, deserts
its premise, and expresses God only in metaphor, therefore it is illogical and the conclusion is not properly drawn. 27
It is logical that because God is Love, Love is divine Prin-

1 ciple; then Love as either divine Principle or Person
stands for God—for both have the nature of God.
3 In logic the major premise must be convertible to the
minor.

In mathematics four times three is twelve, and three
6 times four is twelve. To depart from the rule of mathematics destroys the proof of mathematics; just as a departure from the Principle and rule of divine Science
9 destroys the ability to demonstrate Love according to
Christ, healing the sick; and you lose its susceptibility of
scientific proof.

12 God is the author of Science—neither man nor matter
can be. The Science of God must be, is, *divine*, predi-
cated of Principle and demonstrated as divine Love; and
15 Christianity is divine Science, else there is no Science and
no Christianity.

We understand that God is personal in a scientific
18 sense, but is not corporeal nor anthropomorphic. We understand that God is not finite; He is the infinite Person,
but not three persons in one person. Christian Scientists
21 are theists and monotheists. Those who misjudge us because we understand that God is the infinite One instead
of three, should be able to explain God's personality ra-
24 tionally. Christian Scientists consistently conceive of God
as One because He is infinite; and as triune, because He
is Life, Truth, Love, and these three are one in essence
27 and in office.

If in calling God "divine Principle," meaning divine
Love, more frequently than Person, we merit the epithet
30 "godless," we naturally conclude that he breaks faith with

his creed, or has no possible conception of ours, who be- 1
lieves that three persons are defined strictly by the word
Person, or as One; for if Person is God, and he believes 3
three persons constitute the Godhead, does not Person
here lose the nature of one God, lose monotheism, and
become less coherent than the Christian Scientist's sense 6
of Person as one divine infinite triune Principle, named in
the Bible Life, Truth, Love? — for each of these possesses
the nature of all, and God omnipotent, omnipresent, 9
omniscient.

Man is person; therefore divine metaphysics discrimi-
nates between God and man, the creator and the created, 12
by calling one the divine Principle of all. This suggests
another query: Do Christian Scientists believe in personality? They do, but their personality is defined spiritually, 15
not materially — by Mind, not by matter. We do not blot
out the material race of Adam, but leave all sin to God's
fiat — self-extinction, and to the final manifestation of the 18
real spiritual man and universe. We believe, according
to the Scriptures, that God is infinite Spirit or Person, and
man is His image and likeness: therefore man reflects 21
Spirit, not matter.

We are not transcendentalists to the extent of extin-
guishing anything that is real, good, or true; for God and 24
man in divine Science, or the logic of Truth, are coexistent
and eternal, and the nature of God must be seen in man,
who is His eternal image and likeness. 27

The theological God as a Person necessitates a creed
to explain both His person and nature, whereas God explains Himself in Christian Science. Is the human person, 30

1 as defined by Christian Science, more transcendental than
theology's three divine persons, that live in the Father and
3 have no separate identity? Who says the God of theology
is a Person, and the God of Christian Science is not a
person, hence no God? Here is the departure. Person is
6 defined differently by theology, which reckons three as
one and the infinite in a finite form, and Christian Science,
which reckons one as one and this one *infinite.*

9   Can the infinite Mind inhabit a finite form? Is the God
of theology a finite or an infinite Person? Is He one
Person, or three persons? Who can conceive either of
12 three persons as one person, or of three infinites? We
hear that God is not God except He be a Person, and this
Person contains three persons: yet God must be One
15 although He is three. Is this pure, specific Christianity?
and is God in Christian Science no God because He is not
after this model of personality?

18   The logic of divine Science being faultless, its consequent
Christianity is consistent with Christ's hillside sermon,
which is set aside to some degree, regarded as impracticable
21 for human use, its theory even seldom named.

God is Person in the infinite scientific sense of Him, but
He can neither be one nor infinite in the corporeal or an-
24 thropomorphic sense.

Our departure from theological personality is, that God's
personality must be as infinite as Mind is. We believe in
27 God as the infinite Person; but lose all conceivable idea
of Him as a finite Person with an infinite Mind. That
God is either inconceivable, or is manlike, is not my sense
30 of Him. In divine Science He is "altogether lovely," and

consistently conceivable as the personality of infinite Love, 1
infinite Spirit, than whom there is none other.

Scholastic theology makes God manlike; Christian 3
Science makes man Godlike. The trinity of the Godhead
in Christian Science being Life, Truth, Love, constitutes
the individuality of the infinite Person or divine intelligence 6
called God.

Again, God being infinite Mind, He is the all-wise, all-
knowing, all-loving Father-Mother, for God made man in 9
His own image and likeness, and made them male and
female as the Scriptures declare; then does not our
heavenly Parent — the divine Mind — include within this 12
Mind the thoughts that express the different mentalities
of man and woman, whereby we may consistently say,
"Our Father-Mother God"? And does not this heavenly 15
Parent know and supply the differing needs of the individual mind even as the Scriptures declare He will?

Because Christian Scientists call their God "divine 18
Principle," as well as infinite Person, they have not taken
away their Lord, and know not where they have laid Him.
They do not believe there must be something tangible to 21
the personal material senses in order that belief may attend
their petitions to divine Love. The God whom all Christians now claim to believe in and worship cannot be con- 24
ceived of on that basis; He cannot be apprehended through
the material senses, nor can they gain any evidence of His
presence thereby. Jesus said, "Thomas, because thou 27
hast seen me, thou hast believed: blessed are they that
have not seen, and yet have believed."

1   CHRIST IS ONE AND DIVINE

Again I reiterate this cardinal point: There is but one
3 Christ, and Christ is divine — the Holy Ghost, or spiritual
idea of the divine Principle, Love. Is this scientific statement more transcendental than the belief of our brethren,
6 who regard Jesus as God and the Holy Ghost as the third
person in the Godhead? When Jesus said, "I and my
Father are one," and "my Father is greater than I," this
9 was said in the sense that one ray of light is light, and it
is one with light, but it is not the full-orbed sun. Therefore we have the authority of Jesus for saying Christ is not
12 God, but an impartation of Him.

Again: Is man, according to Christian Science, more
transcendental than God made him? Can he be too spir-
15 itual, since Jesus said, "Be ye therefore perfect, even as
your Father which is in heaven is perfect"? Is God
Spirit? He is. Then is man His image and likeness,
18 according to Holy Writ? He is. Then can man be material, or less than spiritual? As God made man, is he not
wholly spiritual? The reflex image of Spirit is not unlike
21 Spirit. The logic of divine metaphysics makes man none
too transcendental, if we follow the teachings of the
Bible.

24 The Christ was Jesus' spiritual selfhood; therefore
Christ existed prior to Jesus, who said, "Before Abraham
was, I am." Jesus, the only immaculate, was born of a
27 virgin mother, and Christian Science explains that mystic
saying of the Master as to his dual personality, or the spir-

itual and material Christ Jesus, called in Scripture the 1
Son of God and the Son of man — explains it as referring
to his eternal spiritual selfhood and his temporal man- 3
hood. Christian Science shows clearly that God is the
only generating or regenerating power.

The ancient worthies caught glorious glimpses of the 6
Messiah or Christ, and their truer sense of Christ baptized
them in Spirit — submerged them in a sense so pure it
made seers of men, and Christian healers. This is the 9
"Spirit of life in Christ Jesus," spoken of by St. Paul.
It is also the mysticism complained of by the rabbis, who
crucified Jesus and called him a "deceiver." Yea, it is 12
the healing power of Truth that is persecuted to-day, the
spirit of divine Love, and Christ Jesus possessed it, prac-
tised it, and taught his followers to do likewise. This 15
spirit of God is made manifest in the flesh, healing and saving men, — it is the Christ, Comforter, "which taketh away
the sin of the world;" and yet Christ is rejected of men! 18

The evil in human nature foams at the touch of good;
it crieth out, "Let us alone; what have we to do with
thee, . . . ? art thou come to destroy us? I know thee who 21
thou art; the Holy One of God." The Holy Spirit takes
of the things of God and showeth them unto the creature;
and these things being spiritual, they disturb the carnal 24
and destroy it; they are revolutionary, reformatory, and —
now, as aforetime — they cast out evils and heal the sick.
He of God's household who loveth and liveth most the 27
things of Spirit, receiveth them most; he speaketh wisely,
for the spirit of his Father speaketh through him; he
worketh well and healeth quickly, for the spirit giveth him 30

1 liberty: "Ye shall know the truth, and the truth shall make you free."

3 Jesus said, "For all these things they will deliver you up to the councils" and "If they have called the master of the house Beelzebub, how much more shall they call 6 them of his household? Fear them not therefore: for there is nothing covered, that shall not be revealed."

Christ being the Son of God, a spiritual, divine emana- 9 tion, Christ must be spiritual, not material. Jesus was the son of Mary, therefore the son of man only in the sense that man is the generic term for both male and 12 female. The Christ was not human. Jesus was human, but the Christ Jesus represented both the divine and the human, God and man. The Science of divine metaphysics 15 removes the mysticism that used to enthrall my sense of the Godhead, and of Jesus as the Son of God and the son of man. Christian Science explains the nature of God as 18 both Father and Mother.

Theoretically and practically man's salvation comes through "the riches of His grace" in Christ Jesus. Divine 21 Love spans the dark passage of sin, disease, and death with Christ's righteousness, — the atonement of Christ, whereby good destroys evil, — and the victory over self, sin, disease, 24 and death, is won after the pattern of the mount. This is working out our own salvation, for God worketh with us, until there shall be nothing left to perish or to be pun- 27 ished, and we emerge gently into Life everlasting. This is what the Scriptures demand — faith according to works.

30 After Jesus had fulfilled his mission in the flesh as the

Son of man, he rose to the fulness of his stature in Christ, 1
the eternal Son of God, that never suffered and never
died. And because of Jesus' great work on earth, his dem- 3
onstration over sin, disease, and death, the divine nature
of Christ Jesus has risen to human apprehension, and we
see the Son of man in divine Science; and he is no longer 6
a material man, and mind is no longer in matter. Through
this redemptive Christ, Truth, we are healed and saved,
and that not of our selves, it is the gift of God; we are 9
saved from the sins and sufferings of the flesh, and are
the redeemed of the Lord.

THE CHRISTIAN SCIENTISTS' PASTOR   12

   True, I have made the Bible, and "Science and Health
with Key to the Scriptures," the pastor for all the churches
of the Christian Science denomination, but that does not 15
make it impossible for this pastor of ours to preach! To
my sense the Sermon on the Mount, read each Sunday
without comment and obeyed throughout the week, would 18
be enough for Christian practice. The Word of God is a
powerful preacher, and it is not too spiritual to be practical, nor too transcendental to be heard and understood. 21
Whosoever saith there is no sermon without personal
preaching, forgets what Christian Scientists do not, namely,
that God is a Person, and that he should be willing to hear 24
a sermon from his personal God!
   But, my brethren, the Scripture saith, "Answer not a
fool according to his folly, lest thou also be like unto him." 27
St. Paul complains of him whose god is his belly: to

1 such a one our mode of worship may be intangible, for it
is not felt with the fingers; but the spiritual sense drinks
3 it in, and it corrects the material sense and heals the sinning and the sick. If St. John should tell that man that
Jesus came neither eating nor drinking, and that he bap-
6 tized with the Holy Ghost and with fire, he would naturally reply, "That is too transcendental for me to believe,
or for my worship. That is Johnism, and only Johnites
9 would be seen in such company." But this is human: even
the word Christian was anciently an opprobrium; —
hence the Scripture, "When the Son of man cometh, shall
12 he find faith on the earth?"

Though a man were begirt with the Urim and Thum-
mim of priestly office, yet should not have charity, or should
15 deny the validity and permanence of Christ's command to
heal in all ages, he would dishonor that office and misin-
terpret evangelical religion. Divine Science is not an in-
18 terpolation of the Scriptures, it is redolent with health,
holiness, and love. It only needs the prism of divine
Science, which scholastic theology has obscured, to divide
21 the rays of Truth, and bring out the entire hues of God.
The lens of Science magnifies the divine power to human
sight; and we then see the allness of Spirit, therefore the
24 nothingness of matter.

NO REALITY IN EVIL OR SIN

Incorporeal evil embodies itself in the so-called corpo-
27 real, and thus is manifest in the flesh. Evil is neither
quality nor quantity: it is not intelligence, a person or a

66

principle, a man or a woman, a place or a thing, and God 1
never made it. The outcome of evil, called sin, is another
nonentity that belittles itself until it annihilates its own 3
embodiment: this is the only annihilation. The visible
sin should be invisible: it ought not to be seen, felt, or
acted: and because it ought not, we must know it is not, 6
and that sin is a lie from the beginning,—an illusion,
nothing, and only an assumption that nothing is something.
It is not well to maintain the position that sin is sin and 9
can take possession of us and destroy us, but well that we
take possession of sin with such a sense of its nullity as
destroys it. Sin can have neither entity, verity, nor power 12
thus regarded, and we verify Jesus' words, that evil, *alias*
devil, sin, is a lie—therefore is nothing and the father of
nothingness. Christian Science lays the axe at the root of 15
sin, and destroys it on the very basis of nothingness. When
man makes something of sin it is either because he fears it
or loves it. Now, destroy the conception of sin as some- 18
thing, a reality, and you destroy the fear and the love of
it; and sin disappears. A man's fear, unconquered, con-
quers him, in whatever direction.   21

In Christian Science it is plain that God removes the
punishment for sin only as the sin is removed—never
punishes it only as it is destroyed, and never afterwards; 24
hence the hope of universal salvation. It is a sense of sin,
and not a sinful soul, that is lost. Soul is immortal, but
sin is mortal. To lose the sense of sin we must first detect 27
the claim of sin; hold it invalid, give it the lie, and then
we get the victory, sin disappears, and its unreality is
proven. So long as we indulge the presence or believe in 30

1 the power of sin, it sticks to us and has power over us.
Again: To assume there is no reality in sin, and yet com-
3 mit sin, is sin itself, that clings fast to iniquity. The
Publican's wail won his humble desire, while the Phari-
see's self-righteousness crucified Jesus.

6   Do Christian Scientists believe that evil exists? We
answer, Yes and No! Yes, inasmuch as we do know
that evil, as a false claim, false entity, and utter falsity,
9 does exist in thought; and No, as something that enjoys,
suffers, or is *real*. Our only departure from ecclesiasticism on this subject is, that our faith takes hold of the
12 fact that evil cannot be made so real as to frighten us
and so master us, or to make us love it and so hinder our
way to holiness. We regard evil as a lie, an illusion,
15 therefore as unreal as a mirage that misleads the traveller
on his way home.

    It is self-evident that error is not Truth; then it follows
18 that it is untrue; and if untrue, unreal; and if unreal, to
conceive of error as either right or real is sin in itself. To
be delivered from believing in what is unreal, from fear-
21 ing it, following it, or loving it, one must watch and pray
that he enter not into temptation — even as one guards
his door against the approach of thieves. Wrong is
24 thought before it is acted; you must control it in the first
instance, or it will control you in the second. To overcome all wrong, it must become unreal to us: and it is
27 good to know that wrong has no divine authority; therefore man is its master. I rejoice in the scientific apprehension of this grand verity.

30   The evil-doer receives no encouragement from my

declaration that evil is unreal, when I declare that he 1
must awake from his belief in this awful unreality, repent
and forsake it, in order to understand and demonstrate 3
its unreality. Error uncondemned is not nullified. We
must condemn the claim of error in every phase in order
to prove it false, therefore unreal. 6

The Christian Scientist has enlisted to lessen sin, disease, and death, and he overcomes them through Christ,
Truth, teaching him that they cannot overcome us. The 9
resistance to Christian Science weakens in proportion as
one understands it and demonstrates the Science of
Christianity. 12

A sinner ought not to be at ease, or he would never quit
sinning. The most deplorable sight is to contemplate the
infinite blessings that divine Love bestows on mortals, and 15
their ingratitude and hate, filling up the measure of
wickedness against all light. I can conceive of little short
of the old orthodox hell to waken such a one from 18
his deluded sense; for all sin is a deluded sense, and
dis-ease in sin is better than ease. Some mortals may
even need to hear the following thunderbolt of Jonathan 21
Edwards: —

"It is nothing but God's mere pleasure that keeps you
from being this moment swallowed up in everlasting de- 24
struction. He is of purer eyes than to bear to have you in
His sight. There is no other reason to be given why you
have not gone to hell since you have sat here in the house 27
of God, provoking His pure eyes by your sinful, wicked
manner of attending His solemn worship. Yea, there is
nothing else that is to be given as a reason why you do 30

1 not at this moment drop down into hell, but that God's
hand has held you up."

My views of a future and eternal punishment take in a
poignant present sense of sin and its suffering, punishing
6 itself here and hereafter till the sin is destroyed. St.
John's types of sin scarcely equal the modern nonde-
scripts, whereby the demon of this world, its lusts, falsi-
9 ties, envy, and hate, supply sacrilegious gossip with the
verbiage of hades. But hatred gone mad becomes im-
becile — outdoes itself and commits suicide. Then let the
12 dead bury its dead, and surviving defamers share our pity.

In the Greek *devil* is named *serpent — liar — the
god of this world*; and St. Paul defines this world's god as
15 dishonesty, craftiness, handling the word of God deceitfully. The original text defines *devil* as *accuser,
calumniator*; therefore, according to Holy Writ these
18 qualities are objectionable, and ought not to proceed from
the individual, the pulpit, or the press. The Scriptures
once refer to an evil spirit as *dumb*, but in its origin evil
21 was loquacious, and was supposed to outtalk Truth and
to carry a most vital point. Alas! if now it is permitted
license, under sanction of the gown, to handle with gar-
24 rulity age and Christianity! Shall it be said of this century that its greatest discoverer is a woman to whom men
go to mock, and go away to pray? Shall the hope for our
27 race commence with one truth told and one hundred false-
hoods told about it?

The present self-inflicted sufferings of mortals from sin, 1
disease, and death should suffice so to awaken the suf-
ferer from the mortal sense of sin and mind in matter as 3
to cause him to return to the Father's house penitent and
saved; yea, quickly to return to divine Love, the author
and finisher of our faith, who so loves even the repentant 6
prodigal — departed from his better self and struggling
to return — as to meet the sad sinner on his way and to
welcome him home.   9

MEDICINE

Had not my first demonstrations of Christian Science
or metaphysical healing exceeded that of other methods, 12
they would not have arrested public attention and started
the great Cause that to-day commands the respect of our
best thinkers. It was that I healed the deaf, the blind, the 15
dumb, the lame, the last stages of consumption, pneumonia,
etc., and restored the patients in from one to three inter-
views, that started the inquiry, What is it? And when the 18
public sentiment would allow it, and I had overcome a
difficult stage of the work, I would put patients into the
hands of my students and retire from the comparative 21
ease of healing to the next more difficult stage of action
for our Cause.

From my medical practice I had learned that the dynam- 24
ics of medicine is Mind. In the highest attenuations of
homœopathy the drug is utterly expelled, hence it must
be mind that controls the effect; and this attenuation in 27
some cases healed where the allopathic doses would not.

1 When the "mother tincture" of one grain of the drug was
attenuated one thousand degrees less than in the beginning,
3 that was my favorite dose.

The weak criticisms and woeful warnings concerning
Christian Science healing are less now than were the
6 sneers forty years ago at the medicine of homœopathy;
and the medicine of Mind is more honored and respected
to-day than the old-time medicine of matter. Those who
9 laugh at or pray against transcendentalism and the Christian Scientist's religion or his medicine, should know the
danger of questioning Christ Jesus' healing, who admin-
12 istered no remedy apart from Mind, and taught his disciples none other. Christian Science seems transcendental
because the substance of Truth transcends the evidence
15 of the five personal senses, and is discerned only through
divine Science.

If God created drugs for medical use, Jesus and his
18 disciples would have used them and named them for that
purpose, for he came to do "the will of the Father." The
doctor who teaches that a human hypothesis is above a
21 demonstration of healing, yea, above the grandeur of our
great master Metaphysician's precept and example, and
that of his followers in the early centuries, should read
24 this Scripture: "The fool hath said in his heart, There is
no God."

The divine Life, Truth, Love — whom men call God —
27 is the Christian Scientists' healer; and if God destroys the
popular triad — sin, sickness, and death — remember it
is He who does it and so proves their nullity.

30 Christians and clergymen pray for sinners; they believe

that God answers their prayers, and that prayer is a divinely 1
appointed means of grace and salvation. They believe
that divine power, besought, is given to them in times of 3
trouble, and that He worketh with them to save sinners.
I love this doctrine, for I know that prayer brings the
seeker into closer proximity with divine Love, and thus 6
he finds what he seeks, the power of God to heal and to
save. Jesus said, "Ask, and ye shall receive;" and if not
immediately, continue to ask, and because of your often 9
coming it shall be given unto you; and he illustrated his
saying by a parable.

The notion that mixing material and spiritual means, 12
either in medicine or in religion, is wise or efficient, is
proven false. That animal natures give force to character
is egregious nonsense — a flat departure from Jesus' 15
practice and proof. Let us remember that the great Metaphysician healed the sick, raised the dead, and commanded even the winds and waves, which obeyed him 18
through spiritual ascendency alone.

MENTAL MALPRACTICE

From ordinary mental practice to Christian Science is a 21
long ascent, but to go from the use of inanimate drugs to
any susceptible misuse of the human mind, such as mes-
merism, hypnotism, and the like, is to subject mankind 24
unwarned and undefended to the unbridled individual
human will. The currents of God flow through no such
channels.   27

The whole world needs to know that the milder forms

1 of animal magnetism and hypnotism are yielding to its
aggressive features. We have no moral right and no
3 authority in Christian Science for influencing the thoughts
of others, except it be to serve God and benefit mankind.
Man is properly self-governed, and he should be guided
6 by no other mind than Truth, the divine Mind. Christian
Science gives neither moral right nor might to harm either
man or beast. The Christian Scientist is alone with his
9 own being and with the reality of things. The mental
malpractitioner is not, cannot be, a Christian Scientist; he
is disloyal to God and man; he has every opportunity to
12 mislead the human mind, and he uses it. People may
listen complacently to the suggestion of the inaudible
falsehood, not knowing what is hurting them or that they
15 are hurt. This mental bane could not bewilder, darken, or
misguide consciousness, physically, morally, or spiritually,
if the individual knew what was at work and his power
18 over it.

      This unseen evil is the sin of sins; it is never forgiven.
Even the agony and death that it must sooner or later
21 cause the perpetrator, cannot blot out its effects on himself till he suffers up to its extinction and stops practising
it. The crimes committed under this new-old *régime* of
24 necromancy or diabolism are not easily reckoned. At
present its mystery protects it, but its hidden modus and
flagrance will finally be known, and the laws of our land
27 will handle its thefts, adulteries, and murders, and will
pass sentence on the darkest and deepest of human
crimes.

30   Christian Scientists are not hypnotists, they are not

mortal mind-curists, nor faith-curists; they have faith, 1
but they have Science, understanding, and works as well.
They are not the *addenda*, the *et ceteras*, or new editions 3
of old errors; but they are what they are, namely, students of a demonstrable Science leading the ages.

QUESTIONABLE METAPHYSICS 6

In an article published in the *New York Journal*,
Rev.—— writes: "To the famous Bishop Berkeley of the
Church of England may be traced many of the ideas about 9
the spiritual world which are now taught in Christian
Science."

This clergyman gives it as his opinion that Christian 12
Science will be improved in its teaching and authorship
after Mrs. Eddy has gone. I am sorry for my critic, who
reckons hopefully on the death of an individual who loves 15
God and man; such foreseeing is not foreknowing, and
exhibits a startling ignorance of Christian Science, and a
manifest unfitness to criticise it or to compare its literature. 18
He begins his calculation erroneously; for Life is the
Principle of Christian Science and of its results. Death
is neither the predicate nor postulate of Truth, and Christ 21
came not to bring death but life into the world. Does this
critic know of a better way than Christ's whereby to benefit
the race? My faith assures me that God knows more 24
than any man on this subject, for did He not know all
things and results I should not have known Christian
Science, or felt the incipient touch of divine Love which 27
inspired it.

1   That God is good, that Truth is true, and Science is
Science, who can doubt; and whosoever demonstrates the
3 truth of these propositions is to some extent a Christian
Scientist. Is Science material? No! It is the Mind of
God — and God is Spirit. Is Truth material? No!
6 Therefore I do not try to mix matter and Spirit, since
Science does not and they will not mix. I am a spiritual
homœopathist in that I do not believe in such a compound.
9 Truth and Truth is not a compound; Spirit and Spirit is
not: but Truth and error, Spirit and matter, are compounds and opposites; so if one is true, the other is false.
12 If Truth is true, its opposite, error, is not; and if Spirit is
true and infinite, it hath no opposite; therefore matter
cannot be a reality.
15   I begin at the feet of Christ and with the numeration
table of Christian Science. But I do not say that one added
to one is three, or one and a half, nor say this to accom-
18 modate popular opinion as to the Science of Christianity.
I adhere to my text, that one and one are two all the way
up to the infinite calculus of the infinite God. The numer-
21 ation table of Christian Science, its divine Principle and
rules, are before the people, and the different religious
sects and the differing schools of medicine are discussing
24 them as if they understood its Principle and rules before
they have learned its numeration table, and insist that the
public receive their sense of the Science, or that it receive
27 no sense whatever of it.
     Again: Even the numeration table of Christian Science
is not taught correctly by those who have departed from
30 its absolute simple statement as to Spirit and matter, and

that one and two are neither more nor less than three; 1
and losing the numeration table and the logic of Christian
Science, they have little left that the sects and faculties 3
can grapple. If Christian Scientists only would admit
that God is Spirit and infinite, yet that God has an opposite and that the infinite is not all; that God is good and 6
infinite, yet that evil exists and is real, — thence it would
follow that evil must either exist in good, or exist outside
of the *infinite*, — they would be in peace with the 9
schools.

  This departure, however, from the scientific statement,
the divine Principle, rule, or demonstration of Christian 12
Science, results as would a change of the denominations
of mathematics; and you cannot demonstrate Christian
Science except on its fixed Principle and given rule, ac- 15
cording to the Master's teaching and proof. He was ultra;
he was a reformer; he laid the axe at the root of all error,
amalgamation, and compounds. He used no material 18
medicine, nor recommended it, and taught his disciples
and followers to do likewise; therefore he demonstrated
his power over matter, sin, disease, and death, as no other 21
person has ever demonstrated it.

  Bishop Berkeley published a book in 1710 entitled
"Treatise Concerning the Principle of Human Knowl- 24
edge." Its object was to deny, on received principles of
philosophy, the reality of an external material world. In
later publications he declared physical substance to be 27
"only the constant relation between phenomena connected
by association and conjoined by the operations of the
universal mind, nature being nothing more than conscious 30

1 experience. Matter apart from conscious mind is an impossible and unreal concept." He denies the existence of
3 matter, and argues that matter is not *without* the mind,
but within it, and that that which is generally called
matter is only an impression produced by divine power on
6 the mind by means of invariable rules styled the laws of
nature. Here he makes God the cause of all the ills of
mortals and the casualties of earth.

9   Again, while descanting on the virtues of tar-water, he
writes: "I esteem my having taken this medicine the
greatest of all temporal blessings, and am convinced that
12 under Providence I owe my life to it." Making matter
more potent than Mind, when the storms of disease beat
against Bishop Berkeley's metaphysics and personality he
15 fell, and great was the fall — from divine metaphysics to
tar-water!

      Christian Science is more than two hundred years old.
18 It dates beyond Socrates, Leibnitz, Berkeley, Darwin, or
Huxley. It is as old as God, although its earthly advent
is called the Christian era.

21   I had not read one line of Berkeley's writings when I
published my work Science and Health, the Christian
Science textbook.

24   In contradistinction to his views I found it necessary to
follow Jesus' teachings, and none other, in order to
demonstrate the divine Science of Christianity — the meta-
27 physics of Christ — healing all manner of diseases. Philosophy, *materia medica*, and scholastic theology were
inadequate to prove the doctrine of Jesus, and I relin-
30 quished the form to attain the spirit or mystery of

godliness. Hence the mysticism, so called, of my writings   1
becomes clear to the godly.

Building on the rock of Christ's teachings, we have a   3
superstructure eternal in the heavens, omnipotent on earth,
encompassing time and eternity. The stone which the
builders reject is apt to be the cross, which they reject and   6
whereby is won the crown and the head of the corner.

A knowledge of philosophy and of medicine, the scho-
lasticism of a bishop, and the metaphysics (so called)   9
which mix matter and mind, — certain individuals call
aids to divine metaphysics, and regret their lack in my
books, which because of their more spiritual import heal   12
the sick! No Christly axioms, practices, or parables are
alluded to or required in such metaphysics, and the demonstration of matter minus, and God all, ends in some   15
specious folly.

The great Metaphysician, Christ Jesus, denounced all
such gilded sepulchres of his time and of all time. He   18
never recommended drugs, he never used them. What,
then, is our authority in Christianity for metaphysics based
on materialism? He demonstrated what he taught. Had   21
he taught the power of Spirit, and along with this the
power of matter, he would have been as contradictory
as the blending of good and evil, and the latter superior,   24
which Satan demanded in the beginning, and which has
since been avowed to be as real, and matter as useful, as
the infinite God, — good, — which, if indeed Spirit and   27
infinite, excludes evil and matter. Jesus likened such
self-contradictions to a kingdom divided against itself,
that cannot stand.   30

1   The unity and consistency of Jesus' theory and practice
give my tired sense of false philosophy and material the-
3 ology rest. The great teacher, preacher, and demonstrator
of Christianity is the Master, who founded his system of
metaphysics only on Christ, Truth, and supported it by
6 his words and deeds.

   The five personal senses can have only a finite sense
of the infinite: therefore the metaphysician is sensual
9 that combines matter with Spirit. In one sentence he
declaims against matter, in the next he endows it with a
life-giving quality not to be found in God! and turns
12 away from Christ's purely spiritual means to the schools
and matter for help in times of need.

   I have passed through deep waters to preserve Christ's
15 vesture unrent; then, when land is reached and the world
aroused, shall the word popularity be pinned to the seam-
less robe, and they cast lots for it? God forbid! Let
18 it be left to such as see God — to the pure in spirit,
and the meek that inherit the earth; left to them of a
sound faith and charity, the greatest of which is charity
21 — spiritual love. St. Paul said: "Though I speak
with the tongues of men and of angels, and have not
charity, I am become as sounding brass, or a tinkling
24 cymbal."

   Before leaving this subject of the old metaphysicians,
allow me to add I have read little of their writings. I was
27 not drawn to them by a native or an acquired taste for
what was problematic and self-contradictory. What I
have given to the world on the subject of metaphysical
30 healing or Christian Science is the result of my own ob-

servation, experience, and final discovery, quite independ-   1
ent of all other authors except the Bible.

My critic also writes: "The best contributions that   3
have been made to the literature of Christian Science have
been by Mrs. Eddy's followers. I look to see some St.
Paul arise among the Christian Scientists who will inter-   6
pret their ideas and principles more clearly, and apply
them more rationally to human needs."

My works are the first ever published on Christian   9
Science, and nothing has since appeared that is correct
on this subject the basis whereof cannot be traced to some
of those works. The application of Christian Science is   12
healing and reforming mankind. If any one as yet has
healed hopeless cases, such as I have in one to three inter-
views with the patients, I shall rejoice in being informed   15
thereof. Or if a modern St. Paul could start thirty years
ago without a Christian Scientist on earth, and in this
interval number one million, and an equal number of sick   18
healed, also sinners reformed and the habits and appetites of mankind corrected, why was it not done? God is
no respecter of persons.   21

I have put less of my own personality into Christian
Science than others do in proportion, as I have taken out
of its metaphysics all matter and left Christian Science   24
as it is, purely spiritual, Christlike — the Mind of God
and not of man — born of the Spirit and not matter.
Professor Agassiz said: "Every great scientific truth goes   27
through three stages. First, people say it conflicts with
the Bible. Next, they say it has been discovered before.
Lastly, they say they had always believed it." Having   30

1 passed through the first two stages, Christian Science must
be approaching the last stage of the great naturalist's
3 prophecy.

It is only by praying, watching, and working for the
kingdom of heaven within us and upon earth, that we
6 enter the strait and narrow way, whereof our Master said,
"and few there be that find it."

Of the ancient writers since the first century of the
9 Christian era perhaps none lived a more devout Christian
life up to his highest understanding than St. Augustine.
Some of his writings have been translated into almost
12 every Christian tongue, and are classed with the choicest
memorials of devotion both in Catholic and Protestant
oratories.

15 Sacred history shows that those who have followed ex-
clusively Christ's teaching, have been scourged in the
synagogues and persecuted from city to city. But this
18 is no cause for not following it; and my only apology for
trying to follow it is that I love Christ more than all the
world, and my demonstration of Christian Science in
21 healing has proven to me beyond a doubt that Christ,
Truth, is indeed the way of salvation from all that worketh or maketh a lie. As Jesus said: "It is enough for
24 the disciple that he be as his master." It is well to know
that even Christ Jesus, who was not popular among the
worldlings in his age, is not popular with them in this
27 age; hence the inference that he who would be popular
if he could, is not a student of Christ Jesus.

After a hard and successful career reformers usually
30 are handsomely provided for. Has the thought come to

Christian Scientists, Have we housed, fed, clothed, or 1
visited a reformer for that purpose? Have we looked after
or even known of his sore necessities? Gifts he needs not. 3
God has provided the means for him while he was provid-
ing ways and means for others. But mortals in the advancing stages of their careers need the watchful and 6
tender care of those who want to help them. The aged
reformer should not be left to the mercy of those who are
not glad to sacrifice for him even as he has sacrificed for 9
others all the best of his earthly years.

I say this not because reformers are not loved, but because well-meaning people sometimes are inapt or selfish 12
in showing their love. They are like children that go out
from the parents who nurtured them, toiled for them, and
enabled them to be grand coworkers for mankind, children 15
who forget their parents' increasing years and needs, and
whenever they return to the old home go not to help
mother but to recruit themselves. Or, if they attempt 18
to help their parents, and adverse winds are blowing, this
is no excuse for waiting till the wind shifts. They should
remember that mother worked and won for them by 21
facing the winds. All honor and success to those who
honor their father and mother. The individual who loves
most, does most, and sacrifices most for the reformer, is 24
the individual who soonest will walk in his footsteps.

To aid my students in starting under a tithe of my own
difficulties, I allowed them for several years fifty cents on 27
every book of mine that they sold. "With this percentage," students wrote me, "quite quickly we have regained
our tuition for the college course." 30

1   Christian Scientists are persecuted even as all other
religious denominations have been, since ever the primi-
3 tive Christians, "of whom the world was not worthy."
We err in thinking the object of vital Christianity is only
the bequeathing of itself to the coming centuries. The
6 successive utterances of reformers are essential to its
propagation. The magnitude of its meaning forbids head-
long haste, and the consciousness which is most imbued
9 struggles to articulate itself.

   Christian Scientists are practically non-resistants; they
are too occupied with doing good, observing the Golden
12 Rule, to retaliate or to seek redress; they are not quacks,
giving birth to nothing and death to all, — but they are
leaders of a reform in religion and in medicine, and they
15 have no craft that is in danger.

   Even religion and therapeutics need regenerating.
Philanthropists, and the higher class of critics in theology
18 and *materia medica*, recognize that Christian Science
kindles the inner genial life of a man, destroying all lower
considerations. No man or woman is roused to the estab-
21 lishment of a new-old religion by the hope of ease, pleasure,
or recompense, or by the stress of the appetites and passions. And no emperor is obeyed like the man "clouting
24 his own cloak" — working alone with God, yea, like the
clear, far-seeing vision, the calm courage, and the great
heart of the unselfed Christian hero.

27   I counsel Christian Scientists under all circumstances
to obey the Golden Rule, and to adopt Pope's axiom:
"An honest, sensible, and well-bred man will not insult
30 me, and no other can." The sensualist and world-wor-

shipper are always stung by a clear elucidation of truth, 1
of right, and of wrong.

The only opposing element that sects or professions 3
can encounter in Christian Science is Truth opposed to
all error, specific or universal. This opposition springs
from the very nature of Truth, being neither personal nor 6
human, but divine. Every true Christian in the near
future will learn and love the truths of Christian Science
that now seem troublesome. Jesus said, "I came not to 9
send peace but a sword."

Has God entrusted me with a message to mankind? —
then I cannot choose but obey. After a long acquaintance 12
with the communicants of my large church, they regard
me with no vague, fruitless, inquiring wonder. I can use
the power that God gives me in no way except in the 15
interest of the individual and the community. To this
verity every member of my church would bear loving
testimony. 18

MY CHILDHOOD'S CHURCH HOME

Among the list of blessings infinite I count these dear:
Devout orthodox parents; my early culture in the Congre- 21
gational Church; the daily Bible reading and family
prayer; my cradle hymn and the Lord's Prayer, repeated
at night; my early association with distinguished Chris- 24
tian clergymen, who held fast to whatever is good, used
faithfully God's Word, and yielded up graciously what
He took away. It was my fair fortune to be often taught 27
by some grand old divines, among whom were the Rev.

1 Abraham Burnham of Pembroke, N. H., Rev. Nathaniel
Bouton, D. D., of Concord, N. H., Congregationalists;
3 Rev. Mr. Boswell, of Bow, N. H., Baptist; Rev. Enoch
Corser, and Rev. Corban Curtice, Congregationalists; and
Father Hinds, Methodist Elder. I became early a child
6 of the Church, an eager lover and student of vital Christianity. Why I loved Christians of the old sort was I
could not help loving them. Full of charity and good
9 works, busy about their Master's business, they had no
time or desire to defame their fellow-men. God seemed
to shield the whole world in their hearts, and they were
12 willing to renounce all for Him. When infidels assailed
them, however, the courage of their convictions was seen.
They were heroes in the strife; they armed quickly, aimed
15 deadly, and spared no denunciation. Their convictions
were honest, and they lived them; and the sermons their
lives preached caused me to love their doctrines.
18   The lives of those old-fashioned leaders of religion explain in a few words a good man. They fill the ecclesi-
astic measure, that to love God and keep His command-
21 ments is the whole duty of man. Such churchmen and
the Bible, especially the First Commandment of the Decalogue, and Ninety-first Psalm, the Sermon on the Mount,
24 and St. John's Revelation, educated my thought many
years, yea, all the way up to its preparation for and recep-
tion of the Science of Christianity. I believe, if those
27 venerable Christians were here to-day, their sanctified
souls would take in the spirit and understanding of Christian Science through the flood-gates of Love; with them
30 Love was the governing impulse of every action; their

piety was the all-important consideration of their being, the original beauty of holiness that to-day seems to be fading so sensibly from our sight.

To plant for eternity, the "accuser" or "calumniator" must not be admitted to the vineyard of our Lord, and the hand of love must sow the seed. Carlyle writes: "Quackery and dupery do abound in religion; above all, in the more advanced decaying stages of religion, they have fearfully abounded; but quackery was never the originating influence in such things; it was not the health and life of religion, but their disease, the sure precursor that they were about to die."

Christian Scientists first and last ask not to be judged on a doctrinal platform, a creed, or a diploma for scientific guessing. But they do ask to be allowed the rights of conscience and the protection of the constitutional laws of their land; they ask to be known by their works, to be judged (if at all) by their works. We admit that they do not kill people with poisonous drugs, with the lance, or with liquor, in order to heal them. Is it for not killing them thus, or is it for healing them through the might and majesty of divine power after the manner taught by Jesus, and which he enjoined his students to teach and practise, that they are maligned? The richest and most positive proof that a religion in this century is just what it was in the first centuries is that the same reviling it received then it receives now, and from the same motives which actuate one sect to persecute another in advance of it.

Christian Scientists are harmless citizens that do not kill people either by their practice or by preventing the

1 early employment of an M.D. Why? Because the effect
of prayer, whereby Christendom saves sinners, is quite
3 as salutary in the healing of all manner of diseases. The
Bible is our authority for asserting this, in both cases.
The interval that detains the patient from the attendance
6 of an M.D., occupied in prayer and in spiritual obedience
to Christ's mode and means of healing, cannot be fatal
to the patient, and is proven to be more pathological than
9 the M.D.'s material prescription. If this be not so, where
shall we look for the standard of Christianity? Have we
misread the evangelical precepts and the canonical writ-
12 ings of the Fathers, or must we have a new Bible and a
new system of Christianity, originating not in God, but
a creation of the schools — a material religion, proscrip-
15 tive, intolerant, wantonly bereft of the Word of God.

Give us, dear God, again on earth the lost chord of
Christ; solace us with the song of angels rejoicing with
18 them that rejoice; that sweet charity which seeketh not
her own but another's good, yea, which *knoweth no evil.*

Finally, brethren, wait patiently on God; return bless-
21 ing for cursing; be not overcome of evil, but overcome
evil with good; be steadfast, abide and abound in faith,
understanding, and good works; study the Bible and the
24 textbook of our denomination; obey strictly the laws that
be, and follow your Leader only so far as she follows
Christ. Godliness or Christianity is a human necessity:
27 man cannot live without it; he has no intelligence, health,
hope, nor happiness without godliness. In the words of
the Hebrew writers: "Trust in the Lord with all thine
30 heart; and lean not unto thine own understanding. In

all thy ways acknowledge Him, and He shall direct thy   1
paths;" "and He shall bring forth thy righteousness as
the light, and thy judgment as the noonday."   3

The question oft presents itself, Are we willing to sacrifice self for the Cause of Christ, willing to bare our bosom
to the blade and lay ourselves upon the altar? Christian   6
Science appeals loudly to those asleep upon the hill-tops
of Zion. It is a clarion call to the reign of righteousness,
to the kingdom of heaven within us and on earth, and   9
Love is the way alway.

> O the Love divine that plucks us
>   From the human agony!   12
> O the Master's glory won thus,
>   Doth it dawn on you and me?
>
> And the bliss of blotted-out sin   15
>   And the working hitherto —
> Shall we share it — do we walk in
>   Patient faith the way thereto?   18

Message
to
The Mother
Church
June 15, 1902

Message for 1902
The Old and the New Commandment

BELOVED brethren, another year of God's loving providence for His people in times of persecution has marked the history of Christian Science. With no special effort to achieve this result, our church communicants constantly increase in number, unity, steadfastness. Two thousand seven hundred and eighty-four members have been added to our church during the year ending June, 1902, making total twenty-four thousand two hundred and seventy-eight members; while our branch churches are multiplying everywhere and blossoming as the rose. Evil, though combined in formidable conspiracy, is made to glorify God. The Scripture declares, "The wrath of man shall praise Thee: the remainder of wrath shalt Thou restrain."

Whatever seems calculated to displace or discredit the ordinary systems of religious beliefs and opinions wrestling only with material observation, has always met with opposition and detraction; this ought not so to be, for a system that honors God and benefits mankind should be welcomed and sustained. While Christian Science, engaging the attention of philosopher and sage, is circling

1 the globe, only the earnest, honest investigator sees
through the mist of mortal strife this daystar, and whither
3 it guides.

To live and let live, without clamor for distinction or
recognition; to wait on divine Love; to write truth first
6 on the tablet of one's own heart, — this is the sanity and
perfection of living, and my human ideal. The Science
of man and the universe, in contradistinction to all error,
9 is on the way, and Truth makes haste to meet and to welcome it. It is purifying all peoples, religions, ethics, and
learning, and making the children our teachers.

12 Within the last decade religion in the United States has
passed from stern Protestantism to doubtful liberalism.
God speed the right! The wise builders will build on the
15 stone at the head of the corner; and so Christian Science,
the little leaven hid in three measures of meal, — ethics,
medicine, and religion, — is rapidly fermenting, and en-
18 lightening the world with the glory of untrammelled truth.
The present modifications in ecclesiasticism are an outcome of progress; dogmatism, relegated to the past, gives
21 place to a more spiritual manifestation, wherein Christ
is Alpha and Omega. It was an inherent characteristic
of my nature, a kind of birthmark, to love the Church;
24 and the Church once loved me. Then why not remain
friends, or at least agree to disagree, in love, — part fair
foes. I never left the Church, either in heart or in doc-
27 trine; I but began where the Church left off. When the
churches and I round the gospel of grace, in the circle of
love, we shall meet again, never to part. I have always
30 taught the student to overcome evil with good, used no

other means myself; and ten thousand loyal Christian 1
Scientists to one disloyal, bear testimony to this fact.

The loosening cords of non-Christian religions in the 3
Orient are apparent. It is cause for joy that among the
educated classes Buddhism and Shintoism are said to
be regarded now more as a philosophy than as a religion. 6

I rejoice that the President of the United States has put
an end, at Charleston, to any lingering sense of the North's
half-hostility to the South, thus reinstating the old national 9
family pride and joy in the sisterhood of States.

Our nation's forward step was the inauguration of
home rule in Cuba, — our military forces withdrawing, 12
and leaving her in the enjoyment of self-government under
improved laws. It is well that our government, in its brief
occupation of that pearl of the ocean, has so improved her 15
public school system that her dusky children are learning
to read and write.

The world rejoices with our sister nation over the close 18
of the conflict in South Africa; now, British and Boer may
prosper in peace, wiser at the close than the beginning of
war. The dazzling diadem of royalty will sit easier on the 21
brow of good King Edward, — the muffled fear of death
and triumph canker not his coronation, and woman's
thoughts — the joy of the sainted Queen, and the lay of 24
angels — hallow the ring of state.

It does not follow that power must mature into oppres-
sion; indeed, right is the only real potency; and the only 27
true ambition is to serve God and to help the race. Envy
is the atmosphere of hell. According to Holy Writ, the
first lie and leap into perdition began with "Believe in 30

1 me." Competition in commerce, deceit in councils, dishonor in nations, dishonesty in trusts, begin with "Who
3 shall be greatest?" I again repeat, Follow your Leader,
only so far as she follows Christ.

I cordially congratulate our Board of Lectureship, and
6 Publication Committee, on their adequacy and correct
analysis of Christian Science. Let us all pray at this
Communion season for more grace, a more fulfilled life
9 and spiritual understanding, bringing music to the ear,
rapture to the heart — a fathomless peace between
Soul and sense — and that our works be as worthy as
12 our words.

My subject to-day embraces the First Commandment
in the Hebrew Decalogue, and the new commandment in
15 the gospel of peace, both ringing like soft vesper chimes
adown the corridors of time, and echoing and reechoing
through the measureless rounds of eternity.

18   GOD AS LOVE

The First Commandment, "Thou shalt have no other
gods before me," is a law never to be abrogated — a divine
21 statute for yesterday, and to-day, and forever. I shall
briefly consider these two commandments in a few of their
infinite meanings, applicable to all periods — past, present,
24 and future.

Alternately transported and alarmed by abstruse
problems of Scripture, we are liable to turn from them as
27 impractical, or beyond the ken of mortals, — and past
finding out. Our thoughts of the Bible utter our lives.

As silent night foretells the dawn and din of morn; as the
dulness of to-day prophesies renewed energy for to-morrow,
— so the pagan philosophies and tribal religions of yesterday but foreshadowed the spiritual dawn of the twentieth
century — religion parting with its materiality.

Christian Science stills all distress over doubtful inter-
pretations of the Bible; it lights the fires of the Holy
Ghost, and floods the world with the baptism of Jesus.
It is this ethereal flame, this almost unconceived light of
divine Love, that heaven husbands in the First Commandment.

For man to be thoroughly subordinated to this commandment, God must be intelligently considered and
understood. The ever-recurring human question and
wonder, What is God? can never be answered satisfac-
torily by human hypotheses or philosophy. Divine metaphysics and St. John have answered this great question
forever in these words: "God is Love." This absolute
definition of Deity is the theme for time and for eternity;
it is iterated in the law of God, reiterated in the gospel of
Christ, voiced in the thunder of Sinai, and breathed in
the Sermon on the Mount. Hence our Master's saying,
"Think not that I am come to destroy the law, or the
prophets: I am not come to destroy, but to fulfil."

Since God is Love, and infinite, why should mortals
conceive of a law, propound a question, formulate a doctrine, or speculate on the existence of anything which is
an antipode of *infinite* Love and the manifestation thereof?
The sacred command, "Thou shalt have no other gods
before me," silences all questions on this subject, and for-

1 ever forbids the thought of any other reality, since it is impossible to have aught unlike the infinite.

3   The knowledge of life, substance, or law, apart or other
than God — good — is forbidden. The curse of Love
and Truth was pronounced upon a lie, upon false knowl-
6 edge, the fruits of the flesh not Spirit. Since knowledge
of evil, of something besides God, good, brought death
into the world on the basis of a lie, Love and Truth de-
9 stroy this knowledge, — and Christ, Truth, demonstrated
and continues to demonstrate this grand verity, saving
the sinner and healing the sick. Jesus said a lie fathers
12 itself, thereby showing that God made neither evil nor its
consequences. Here all human woe is seen to obtain in
a false claim, an untrue consciousness, an impossible
15 creation, yea, something that is not of God. The Chris-
tianization of mortals, whereby the mortal concept and
all it includes is obliterated, lets in the divine sense of
18 being, fulfils the law in righteousness, and consummates
the First Commandment, "Thou shalt have no other gods
before me." All Christian faith, hope, and prayer, all
21 devout desire, virtually petition, Make me the image and
likeness of divine Love.

   Through Christ, Truth, divine metaphysics points the
24 way, demonstrates heaven here, — the struggle over, and
victory on the side of Truth. In the degree that man becomes spiritually minded he becomes Godlike. St. Paul
27 writes: "For to be carnally minded is death; but to be
spiritually minded is life and peace." Divine Science
fulfils the law and the gospel, wherein God is infinite Love,
30 including nothing unlovely, producing nothing unlike

Himself, the true nature of Love intact and eternal. Divine 1
metaphysics concedes no origin or causation apart from
God. It accords all to God, Spirit, and His infinite mani- 3
festations of love — man and the universe.

In the first chapter of Genesis, matter, sin, disease, and
death enter not into the category of creation or conscious- 6
ness. Minus this spiritual understanding of Scripture, of
God and His creation, neither philosophy, nature, nor
grace can give man the true idea of God — divine Love — 9
sufficiently to fulfil the First Commandment.

The Latin *omni*, which signifies *all*, used as an English
prefix to the words *potence, presence, science*, signifies all- 12
power, all-presence, all-science. Use these words to define
God, and nothing is left to consciousness but Love, without
beginning and without end, even the forever *I* AM, and 15
All, than which there is naught else. Thus we have
Scriptural authority for divine metaphysics — spiritual
man and the universe coexistent with God. No other 18
logical conclusion can be drawn from the premises,
and no other scientific proposition can be Christianly
entertained. 21

LOVE ONE ANOTHER

Here we proceed to another Scriptural passage which
serves to confirm Christian Science. Christ Jesus saith, 24
"A new commandment I give unto you, That ye love one
another; as I have loved you." It is obvious that he
called his disciples' special attention to his *new command-* 27
ment. And wherefore? Because it emphasizes the

99

1 apostle's declaration, "God is Love," — it elucidates
Christianity, illustrates God, and man as His likeness, and
3 commands man to love as Jesus loved.

The law and the gospel concur, and both will be fulfilled. Is it necessary to say that the likeness of God, Spirit,
6 is spiritual, and the likeness of Love is loving? When
loving, we learn that "God is Love;" mortals hating, or
unloving, are neither Christians nor Scientists. The new
9 commandment of Christ Jesus shows what true spirituality
is, and its harmonious effects on the sick and the sinner.
No person can heal or reform mankind unless he is actuated
12 by love and good will towards men. The coincidence between the law and the gospel, between the old and the new
commandment, confirms the fact that God and Love are
15 *one*. The spiritually minded are inspired with tenderness,
Truth, and Love. The life of Christ Jesus, his words and
his deeds, demonstrate Love. We have no evidence of
18 being Christian Scientists except we possess this inspiration, and its power to heal and to save. The energy that
saves sinners and heals the sick is divine: and Love is the
21 Principle thereof. Scientific Christianity works out the
rule of spiritual love; it makes man *active*, it prompts per-
petual goodness, for the ego, or I, goes to the Father,
24 whereby man *is* Godlike. Love, purity, meekness, coexist in divine Science. Lust, hatred, revenge, coincide in
material sense. Christ Jesus reckoned man in Science,
27 having the kingdom of heaven within him. He spake of
man not as the offspring of Adam, a departure from God,
or His lost likeness, but as God's child. Spiritual love
30 makes man conscious that God is his Father, and the con-

sciousness of God as Love gives man power with untold 1
furtherance. Then God becomes to him the All-presence
— quenching sin; the All-power — giving life, health, 3
holiness; the All-science — all law and gospel.

Jesus commanded, "Follow me; and let the dead bury
their dead;" in other words, Let the world, popularity, 6
pride, and ease concern you less, and *love thou.* When
the full significance of this saying is understood, we shall
have better practitioners, and Truth will arise in human 9
thought with healing in its wings, regenerating mankind
and fulfilling the apostle's saying: "For the law of the
Spirit of life in Christ Jesus hath made me free from the 12
law of sin and death." Loving chords set discords in harmony. Every condition implied by the great Master,
every promise fulfilled, was loving and spiritual, urging 15
a state of consciousness that leaves the minor tones of so-
called material life and abides in Christlikeness.

The unity of God and man is not the dream of a heated 18
brain; it is the spirit of the healing Christ, that dwelt forever in the bosom of the Father, and should abide forever
in man. When first I heard the life-giving sound thereof, 21
and knew not whence it came nor whither it tended, it
was the proof of its divine origin, and healing power, that
opened my closed eyes. 24

Did the age's thinkers laugh long over Morse's discovery of telegraphy? Did they quarrel long with the
inventor of a steam engine? Is it cause for bitter com- 27
ment and personal abuse that an individual has met the
need of mankind with some new-old truth that counteracts
ignorance and superstition? Whatever enlarges man's 30

1 facilities for knowing and doing good, and subjugates
matter, has a fight with the flesh. Utilizing the capacities
3 of the human mind uncovers new ideas, unfolds spiritual
forces, the divine energies, and their power over matter,
molecule, space, time, mortality; and mortals cry out,
6 "Art thou come hither to torment us before the time?"
then dispute the facts, call them false or in advance of the
time, and reiterate, Let me alone. Hence the foot-
9 prints of a reformer are stained with blood. Rev. Hugh
Black writes truly: "The birthplace of civilization is not
Athens, but Calvary."

12   When the human mind is advancing above itself towards
the Divine, it is subjugating the body, subduing matter,
taking steps outward and upwards. This upward ten-
15 dency of humanity will finally gain the scope of Jacob's
vision, and rise from sense to Soul, from earth to heaven.

Religions in general admit that man becomes finally
18 spiritual. If such is man's ultimate, his predicate tending
thereto is correct, and inevitably spiritual. Wherefore,
then, smite the reformer who finds the more spiritual way,
21 shortens the distance, discharges burdensome baggage,
and increases the speed of mortals' transit from matter
to Spirit — yea, from sin to holiness? This is indeed our
24 sole proof that Christ, Truth, is the way. The old and
recurring martyrdom of God's best witnesses is the in-
firmity of evil, the *modus operandi* of human error,
27 carnality, opposition to God and His power in man.
Persecuting a reformer is like sentencing a man for com-
municating with foreign nations in other ways than by
30 walking every step over the land route, and swimming the

ocean with a letter in his hand to leave on a foreign shore. 1
Our heavenly Father never destined mortals who seek
for a better country to wander on the shores of time dis- 3
appointed travellers, tossed to and fro by adverse circumstances, inevitably subject to sin, disease, and death.
Divine Love waits and pleads to save mankind — and 6
awaits with warrant and welcome, grace and glory, the
earth-weary and heavy-laden who find and point the path
to heaven.   9

Envy or abuse of him who, having a new idea or a more
spiritual understanding of God, hastens to help on his
fellow-mortals, is neither Christian nor Science. If a 12
postal service, a steam engine, a submarine cable, a wire-
less telegraph, each in turn has helped mankind, how
much more is accomplished when the race is helped on- 15
ward by a new-old message from God, even the knowledge of salvation from sin, disease, and death.

The world's wickedness gave our glorified Master a 18
bitter cup — which he drank, giving thanks, then gave
it to his followers to drink. Therefore it is thine, advancing Christian, and this is thy Lord's benediction upon 21
it: "Blessed are ye, when men shall revile you, and persecute you, and shall say all manner of evil against you
falsely, for my sake. Rejoice, and be exceeding glad: 24
for great is your reward in heaven: for so persecuted they
the prophets which were before you."

Of old the Jews put to death the Galilean Prophet, the 27
best Christian on earth, for the truths he said and did:
while to-day Jew and Christian can unite in doctrine and in
practice on the very basis of his words and works. The Jew 30

1 believes that the Messiah or the Christ has not yet come;
the Christian believes that Christ is come and is God.
3 Here Christian Science intervenes, explains these doctrinal
points, cancels the disagreement, and settles the whole question on the basis that Christ is the Messiah, the true spir-
6 itual idea, and this ideal of God is *now* and *forever, here* and
everywhere. The Jew who believes in the First Commandment is a monotheist, he has one omnipresent God: thus
9 the Jew unites with the Christian idea that God is come,
and is ever present. The Christian who believes in the
First Commandment is a monotheist: thus he virtually
12 unites with the Jew's belief in one God, and that Jesus
Christ is not God, as he himself declared, but is the Son of
God. This declaration of Christ, understood, conflicts not
15 at all with another of his sayings: "I and my Father are
one," — that is, one in quality, not in quantity. As a drop
of water is one with the ocean, a ray of light one with the
18 sun, even so God and man, Father and son, are one in
being. The Scripture reads: "For in Him we live, and
move, and have our being."
21   Here allow me to interpolate some matters of business
that ordinarily find no place in my Message. It is a privilege to acquaint communicants with the financial transac-
24 tions of this church, so far as I know them, and especially
before making another united effort to purchase more land
and enlarge our church edifice so as to seat the large number
27 who annually favor us with their presence on Communion
Sunday.
    When founding the institutions and early movements of
30 the Cause of Christian Science, I furnished the money from

my own private earnings to meet the expenses involved. 1
In this endeavor self was forgotten, peace sacrificed, Christ
and our Cause my only incentives, and each success in- 3
curred a sharper fire from enmity.

During the last seven years I have transferred to The
Mother Church, of my personal property and funds, to the 6
value of about one hundred and twenty thousand dollars;
and the net profits from the business of The Christian Science Publishing Society (which was a part of this transfer) 9
yield this church a liberal income. I receive no personal
benefit therefrom except the privilege of publishing my
books in their publishing house, and desire none other. 12

The land on which to build The First Church of Christ,
Scientist, in Boston, had been negotiated for, and about one
half the price paid, when a loss of funds occurred, and I 15
came to the rescue, purchased the mortgage on the lot
corner of Falmouth and Caledonia (now Norway) Streets;
paying for it the sum of $4,963.50 and interest, through my 18
legal counsel. After the mortgage had expired and the note
therewith became due, legal proceedings were instituted by
my counsel advertising the property in the Boston news- 21
papers, and giving opportunity for those who had previously
negotiated for the property to redeem the land by paying
the amount due on the mortgage. But no one offering 24
the price I had paid for it, nor to take the property off my
hands, the mortgage was foreclosed, and the land legally
conveyed to me, by my counsel. This land, now valued at 27
twenty thousand dollars, I afterwards gave to my church
through trustees, who were to be known as "The Christian
Science Board of Directors." A copy of this deed is pub- 30

1 lished in our Church Manual. About five thousand dollars
had been paid on the land when I redeemed it. The only
3 interest I retain in this property is to save it for my church.
I can neither rent, mortgage, nor sell this church edifice nor
the land whereon it stands.

6   I suggest as a motto for every Christian Scientist, — a
living and life-giving spiritual shield against the powers of
darkness, —

9   "Great not like Cæsar, stained with blood,
           But only great as I am good."

The only genuine success possible for any Christian — and
12 the only success I have ever achieved — has been accomplished on this solid basis. The remarkable growth and
prosperity of Christian Science are its legitimate fruit. A
15 successful end could never have been compassed on any
other foundation, — with truths so counter to the common
convictions of mankind to present to the world. From the
18 beginning of the great battle every forward step has been
met (not by mankind, but by a kind of men) with mockery,
envy, rivalry, and falsehood — as achievement after achieve-
21 ment has been blazoned on the forefront of the world and
recorded in heaven. The popular philosophies and religions have afforded me neither favor nor protection in the
24 great struggle. Therefore, I ask: What has shielded and
prospered preeminently our great Cause, but the outstretched arm of infinite Love? This pregnant question,
27 answered frankly and honestly, should forever silence all
private criticisms, all unjust public aspersions, and afford
an open field and fair play.

In the eighties, anonymous letters mailed to me con- 1
tained threats to blow up the hall where I preached; yet I
never lost my faith in God, and neither informed the police 3
of these letters nor sought the protection of the laws of my
country. I leaned on God, and was safe.

Healing all manner of diseases without charge, keeping 6
a free institute, rooming and boarding indigent students
that I taught "without money and without price," I strug-
gled on through many years; and while dependent on the 9
income from the sale of Science and Health, my publisher
paid me not one dollar of royalty on its first edition. Those
were days wherein the connection between justice and be- 12
ing approached the mythical. Before entering upon my
great life-work, my income from literary sources was ample,
until, declining dictation as to what I should write, I became 15
poor for Christ's sake. My husband, Colonel Glover, of
Charleston, South Carolina, was considered wealthy, but
much of his property was in slaves, and I declined to sell 18
them at his decease in 1844, for I could never believe that a
human being was my property.

Six weeks I waited on God to suggest a name for the book 21
I had been writing. Its title, Science and Health, came to
me in the silence of night, when the steadfast stars watched
over the world, — when slumber had fled, — and I rose 24
and recorded the hallowed suggestion. The following day
I showed it to my literary friends, who advised me to drop
both the book and the title. To this, however, I gave no 27
heed, feeling sure that God had led me to write that book,
and had whispered that name to my waiting hope and
prayer. It was to me the "still, small voice" that came to 30

107

1 Elijah after the earthquake and the fire. Six months there-
after Miss Dorcas Rawson of Lynn brought to me Wyclif's
3 translation of the New Testament, and pointed out that
identical phrase, "Science and Health," which is rendered
in the Authorized Version "knowledge of salvation."
6 This was my first inkling of Wyclif's use of that combina-
tion of words, or of their rendering. To-day I am the happy
possessor of a copy of Wyclif, the invaluable gift of two
9 Christian Scientists, — Mr. W. Nicholas Miller, K.C., and
Mrs. F. L. Miller, of London, England.

GODLIKENESS

12   St. Paul writes: "Follow peace with all men, and holiness, without which no man shall see the Lord." To attain
peace and holiness is to recognize the divine presence and
15 allness. Jesus said: "I am the way." Kindle the watch-
fires of unselfed love, and they throw a light upon the un-
complaining agony in the life of our Lord; they open the
18 enigmatical seals of the angel, standing in the sun, a glorified spiritual idea of the ever-present God — in whom there
is no darkness, but all is light, and man's immortal being.
21 The meek might, sublime patience, wonderful works, and
opening not his mouth in self-defense against false witnesses, express the life of Godlikeness. Fasting, feasting,
24 or penance, — merely outside forms of religion, — fail to
elucidate Christianity: they reach not the heart nor reno-
vate it; they never destroy one iota of hypocrisy, pride,
27 self-will, envy, or hate. The mere form of godliness,

coupled with selfishness, worldliness, hatred, and lust, are 1
knells tolling the burial of Christ.

Jesus said, "If ye love me, keep my commandments." 3
He knew that obedience is the test of love; that one gladly
obeys when obedience gives him happiness. Selfishly, or
otherwise, all are ready to seek and obey what they love. 6
When mortals learn to love aright; when they learn that
man's highest happiness, that which has most of heaven in
it, is in blessing others, and self-immolation — they will 9
obey both the old and the new commandment, and receive
the reward of obedience.

Many sleep who should keep themselves awake and 12
waken the world. Earth's actors change earth's scenes;
and the curtain of human life should be lifted on reality, on
that which outweighs time; on duty done and life perfected, 15
wherein joy is real and fadeless. Who of the world's lovers
ever found her true? It is wise to be willing to wait on God,
and to be wiser than serpents; to hate no man, to love one's 18
enemies, and to square accounts with each passing hour.
Then thy gain outlives the sun, for the sun shines but to
show man the beauty of holiness and the wealth of love. 21
Happiness consists in being and in doing good; only what
God gives, and what we give ourselves and others through
His tenure, confers happiness: conscious worth satisfies 24
the hungry heart, and nothing else can. Consult thy every-
day life; take its answer as to thy aims, motives, fondest
purposes, and this oracle of years will put to flight all care 27
for the world's soft flattery or its frown. Patience and res-
ignation are the pillars of peace that, like the sun beneath
the horizon, cheer the heart susceptible of light with prom- 30

1 ised joy. Be faithful at the temple gate of conscience,
wakefully guard it; then thou wilt know when the thief
3 cometh.

The constant spectacle of sin thrust upon the pure sense
of the immaculate Jesus made him a man of sorrows. He
6 lived when mortals looked ignorantly, as now, on the might
of divine power manifested through man; only to mock,
wonder, and perish. Sad to say, the cowardice and self-
9 seeking of his disciples helped crown with thorns the life of
him who broke not the bruised reed and quenched not the
smoking flax, — who caused not the feeble to fall, nor
12 spared through false pity the consuming tares. Jesus was
compassionate, true, faithful to rebuke, ready to forgive.
He said, "Inasmuch as ye have done it unto one of the
15 least of these my brethren, ye have done it unto me."
"Love one another, as I have loved you." No estrange-
ment, no emulation, no deceit, enters into the heart that
18 loves as Jesus loved. It is a false sense of love that, like
the summer brook, soon gets dry. Jesus laid down his life
for mankind; what more could he do? Beloved, how much
21 of what he did are we doing? Yet he said, "The works
that I do shall he do." When this prophecy of the great
Teacher is fulfilled we shall have more effective healers and
24 less theorizing; faith without proof loses its life, and it
should be buried. The ignoble conduct of his disciples
towards their Master, showing their unfitness to follow
27 him, ended in the downfall of genuine Christianity, about
the year 325, and the violent death of all his disciples save
one.

30   The nature of Jesus made him keenly alive to the

injustice, ingratitude, treachery, and brutality that he 1
received. Yet behold his love! So soon as he burst the
bonds of the tomb he hastened to console his unfaithful 3
followers and to disarm their fears. Again: True to his
divine nature, he rebuked them on the eve of his ascension,
called one a "fool" — then, lifting up his hands and bless- 6
ing them, he rose from earth to heaven.

The Christian Scientist cherishes no resentment; he
knows that that would harm him more than all the malice 9
of his foes. Brethren, even as Jesus forgave, forgive thou.
I say it with joy, — no person can commit an offense
against me that I cannot forgive. Meekness is the armor 12
of a Christian, his shield and his buckler. He entertains
angels who listens to the lispings of repentance seen in a
tear — happier than the conqueror of a world. To the 15
burdened and weary, Jesus saith: "Come unto me."
O glorious hope! there remaineth a rest for the righteous,
a rest in Christ, a peace in Love. The thought of it stills 18
complaint; the heaving surf of life's troubled sea foams
itself away, and underneath is a deep-settled calm.

Are earth's pleasures, its ties and its treasures, taken 21
away from you? It is divine Love that doeth it, and
sayeth, "Ye have need of all these things." A danger
besets thy path? — a spiritual behest, in reversion, awaits 24
you.

The great Master triumphed in furnace fires. Then,
Christian Scientists, trust, and trusting, you will find divine 27
Science glorifies the cross and crowns the association with
our Saviour in his life of love. There is no redundant
drop in the cup that our Father permits us. Christ 30

1 walketh over the wave; on the ocean of events, mounting
the billow or going down into the deep, the voice of him
3 who stilled the tempest saith, "It is I; be not afraid."
Thus he bringeth us into the desired haven, the kingdom
of Spirit; and the hues of heaven, tipping the dawn of
6 everlasting day, joyfully whisper, "No drunkards within,
no sorrow, no pain; and the glory of earth's woes is risen
upon you, rewarding, satisfying, glorifying thy unfaltering
9 faith and good works with the fulness of divine Love."

'T was God who gave that word of might
Which swelled creation's lay, —
12 "Let there be light, and there was light," —
That swept the clouds away;
'T was Love whose finger traced aloud
15 A bow of promise on the cloud.

Beloved brethren, are you ready to join me in this proposition, namely, in 1902 to begin omitting our *annual*
18 gathering at Pleasant View, — thus breaking any seeming
connection between the sacrament in our church and a
pilgrimage to Concord? I shall be the loser by this change,
21 for it gives me great joy to look into the faces of my dear
church-members; but in this, as all else, I can bear the
cross, while gratefully appreciating the privilege of meet-
24 ing you all *occasionally* in the metropolis of my native
State, whose good people welcome Christian Scientists.

Message
to
The Mother
Church
June 10, 1906

"Choose Ye"

"Choose Ye"

MESSAGE FROM MARY BAKER EDDY ON THE OCCASION   1
OF THE DEDICATION OF THE EXTENSION OF THE
MOTHER CHURCH OF CHRIST, SCIENTIST, JUNE 10, 1906   3

MY BELOVED BRETHREN:—The divine might of
Truth demands well-doing in order to demonstrate truth, and this not alone in accord with human   6
desire but with spiritual power. St. John writes: "Blessed
are they that do His commandments, that they may have
right to the tree of life, and may enter in through the gates   9
into the city." The sear leaves of faith without works,
scattered abroad in Zion's waste places, appeal to reformers, "Show me thy faith by thy works."   12
  Christian Science is not a dweller apart in royal solitude;
it is not a law of matter, nor a transcendentalism that
heals only the sick. This Science is a law of divine Mind,   15
a persuasive animus, an unerring impetus, an ever-present
help. Its presence is felt, for it acts and acts wisely,
always unfolding the highway of hope, faith, understand-   18
ing. It is the higher criticism, the higher hope; and its
effect on man is mainly this—that the good which has
come into his life, examination compels him to think   21
genuine, whoever did it. A Christian Scientist verifies
his calling. *Choose ye!*

115

1   When, by losing his faith in matter and sin, one finds
the spirit of Truth, then he practises the Golden Rule
3 spontaneously;   and obedience to this rule spiritualizes
man, for the world's *nolens volens* cannot enthrall it.
Lust, dishonesty, sin, disable the student; they preclude
6 the practice or efficient teaching of Christian Science, the
truth of man's being. The Scripture reads: "He that
taketh not his cross, and followeth after me, is not worthy
9 of me." On this basis, how many are following the
Way-shower? We follow Truth only as we follow truly,
meekly, patiently, spiritually, blessing saint and sinner
12 with the leaven of divine Love which woman has put
into Christendom and medicine.

A genuine Christian Scientist loves Protestant and
15 Catholic, D.D. and M.D., — loves all who love God,
good; and he loves his enemies. It will be found that,
instead of opposing, such an individual subserves the
18 interests of both medical faculty and Christianity, and
they thrive together, learning that Mind-power is good
will towards men. Thus unfolding the true metal in
21 character, the iron in human nature rusts away; honesty
and justice characterize the seeker and finder of Christian
Science.

24   The pride of place or power is the prince of this world
that hath nothing in Christ. Our great Master said:
"Except ye . . . become as little children, ye shall not
27 enter into the kingdom of heaven," — the reign of righteousness, the glory of good, healing the sick and saving
the sinner. The height of my hope must remain. Glory
30 be to Thee, Thou God most high and nigh.

Whatever is not divinely natural and demonstrably
true, in ethics, philosophy, or religion, is not of God but

116

originates in the minds of mortals. It is the Adam- 1
dream according to the Scriptural allegory, in which
man is supposed to start from dust and woman to be 3
the outcome of man's rib, — marriage synonymous with
legalized lust, and the offspring of sense the murderers
of their brothers!   6

Wholly apart from this mortal dream, this illusion and
delusion of sense, Christian Science comes to reveal man
as God's image, His idea, coexistent with Him — God 9
giving all and man having all that God gives. Whence,
then, came the creation of matter, sin, and death, mortal
pride and power, prestige or privilege? The First Com- 12
mandment of the Hebrew Decalogue, "Thou shalt have
no other gods before me," and the Golden Rule are the
all-in-all of Christian Science. They are the spiritual 15
idealism and realism which, when realized, constitute a
Christian Scientist, heal the sick, reform the sinner, and
rob the grave of its victory. The spiritual understanding 18
which demonstrates Christian Science, enables the devout
Scientist to worship, not an unknown God, but Him whom,
understanding even in part, he continues to love more and 21
to serve better.

Beloved, I am not with you *in propria persona* at this
memorable dedication and communion season, but I am 24
with you "in spirit and in truth," lovingly thanking your
generosity and fidelity, and saying virtually what the
prophet said: Continue to choose whom ye will serve. 27

Forgetting the Golden Rule and indulging sin, men
cannot serve God; they cannot demonstrate the omnipotence of divine Mind that heals the sick and the sinner. 30
Human will may mesmerize and mislead man; divine
wisdom, never. Indulging deceit is like the defendant

1 arguing for the plaintiff in favor of a decision which the defendant knows will be turned against himself.

3 We cannot serve two masters. Do we love God supremely? Are we honest, just, faithful? Are we true to ourselves? "God is not mocked: for whatsoever a
6 man soweth, that shall he also reap." To abide in our unselfed better self is to be done forever with the sins of the flesh, the wrongs of human life, the tempter and
9 temptation, the smile and deceit of damnation. When we have overcome sin in all its forms, men may revile us and despitefully use us, and we shall rejoice, "for great
12 is [our] reward in heaven."

You have dexterously and wisely provided for The Mother Church of Christ, Scientist, a magnificent tem-
15 ple wherein to enter and pray. Greatly impressed and encouraged thereby, deeply do I thank you for this proof of your progress, unity, and love. The modest edifice
18 of The Mother Church of Christ, Scientist, began with the cross; its excelsior extension is the crown. The room of your Leader remains in the beginning of this edifice,
21 evidencing the praise of babes and the word which proceedeth out of the mouth of God. Its crowning ultimate rises to a mental monument, a superstructure high
24 above the work of men's hands, even the outcome of their hearts, giving to the material a spiritual significance — the speed, beauty, and achievements of goodness.
27 Methinks this church is the one edifice on earth which most prefigures self-abnegation, hope, faith; love catching a glimpse of glory.

(*The First Church of Christ, Scientist, and Miscellany,*
pages 3–6)